What Are You Doing  There?

Also by

Charlene C. Giannetti and

Margaret Sagarese

Cliques

The Roller-Coaster Years

Parenting 911

The Patience of a Saint

What Are You Doing **in** There?

Balancing Your Need

to Know with Your Child's

Need to Grow

Charlene C. Giannetti

and Margaret Sagarese

Broadway Books / New York

BROADWAY

PRINTED IN THE UNITED STATES OF AMERICA

BROADWAY BOOKS and its logo, a letter B bisected on the
diagonal, are trademarks of Random House, Inc.

Visit our website at www.broadwaybooks.com

First edition published 2003

Book design by Laurie Jewell

Library of Congress Cataloging-in-Publication Data

Giannetti, Charlene C.
    What are you doing in there? : balancing your need to
know with your child's need to grow   /   by Charlene C.
Giannetti and Margaret Sagarese.
        p.   cm.
    1. Child rearing—United States.   2. Parent and child—
United States.   3. Communication in the family—United
States.   I. Sagarese, Margaret.   II. Title.

HQ769 .G444 2002
649'.1—dc21

                                        2002035033

ISBN 0-7679-1297-7

10 9 8 7 6 5 4 3 2 1

For John Lounsbury,

father of the middle school

movement and premier advocate

for young adolescents,

for his knowledge, inspiration,

support, and friendship.

Contents

Acknowledgments

We can hardly believe that this is our fifth parenting book! We owe a debt of gratitude to all those who have contributed to our efforts.

We want to send a heartfelt thank you to all the parents and teachers, administrators and health professionals who have bought our previous books. Because of your support, both emotional (your compliments and warm wishes) and financial (your going out and buying our books and coming to our lectures), our career has flourished.

When we decided to explore the issue of privacy, once again we tapped into the pulse of parents, educators, and young adolescents who willingly shared with us their secret thoughts and sensitive insights. We appreciate your confidences.

To our new editor at Broadway Books, Patricia Medved, thanks for caring and guiding us to find just the right format and the best positive voice to deliver our message. We hope you tuck away a boxed set for when Amelia hits puberty. Thanks to Gerry Howard for his support and for his astute input that inspired our title. We have said this before, but thank you to everyone at Broadway Books who continually helps us publicize, market, distribute, and sell our books, especially Alana Watkins and Wanda Knight.

A special note of gratitude goes out to the National Middle School Association, especially to Doug Herlensky and Jack Berckemeyer, for helping us reach their network of educators coast to coast.

Without our agent, Denise Marcil, we'd be lost and immobilized somewhere between insecurity and ambition. Thanks, Denise, for keeping us real and productive.

Finally, we thank our families, our husbands Tom and Michael, and our children: Joseph, Theresa (who wrote the IM conversation in the Internet chapter), and Skyler Rose. Our own adolescents (like yours) are a source of inspiration and pleasure, passion and sometimes pain—but isn't that the essence of life and parenting? We think so. We thoroughly enjoyed writing about parenting young adolescents once again, and we hope you enjoy our latest.

—Charlene C. Giannetti and Margaret Sagarese

Introduction

We leaned forward over the wooden cafeteria table separating us from the hushed tones of the eleven- and twelve-year-olds venting at us. In soft tones we probed. Several of the young adolescents fidgeted. A pair of paranoid eyes looked over a shoulder. Apparently speaking so honestly within earshot of authority figures felt risky. No one wanted this covert conversation to be overheard.

What were they whispering about? Their right to privacy and how the adults in their lives trample all over it. One twelve-year-old girl fumed, "It's my life, not theirs!" Another seconded the emotion. "My parents don't need to know everything about my life because they are not God."

Do children have a right to privacy? What about young and older adolescents? Are adolescents entitled to secrets? Yes, so long as those secrets don't create a dangerous secret life. Do parents have the right to rifle through a son and daughter's personal possessions? Should the contents of a girl's pocketbook be off-limits for a parent? And what about the stuff in a boy's backpack or an older adolescent's pockets?

Parade magazine (June 30, 2002) asked teens, "If there was a 'Teen Bill of Rights,' what would you include?" Number one on the list (not surprising to us)—"The right of teenagers to be secure in their persons, rooms, diaries and effects against unreasonable searches and seizures." Furthermore, many deciphered parents' sneaky maneuvers because the statement continued, "No warrants shall be issued upon false pretenses, such as collecting dirty laundry from our room."

While impulses to search and spy on your child are completely understandable, and may seem justifiable, the purpose of this book is to explain why you, as a parent, *don't* need to engage in covert tactics. To snoop or not to snoop is a timely and controversial urge. By the time you get to the last page in this book, you will have information and an agenda that can satisfy you and your children. As we travel through a host of situations, insights, and experiences, we will sort through just how complicated this whole privacy debate is. For example:

Suppose a mother suspects that her son is having sex with his girlfriend. Is she being responsible if she searches for condoms in his wallet or his bureau drawers?

Suppose a parent's alarm bell rings every time her daughter walks through the door in a wafting cloud of cigarette smoke. Is she compelled to hunt for Marlboro Lights?

Suppose a father takes an instant dislike to his son's friends. Is he correct in eavesdropping on their conversations?

Suppose a mother can't explain all the new clothes her daughter's friend brings home from the mall and she wonders about shoplifting. Is she wrong to do a little Old Navy surveillance, tailing the girls on their next shopping trip?

Suppose a teenager seems too melancholy and won't open up. Is it a parent's obligation to break and enter her diary?

You get our drift. Young adolescents are notorious for keeping things from parents. Not coincidentally, mothers and fathers are becoming more and more notorious for trying to crack the barriers.

Over the last decade as we penned four parenting books delving into the life and times of ten- to fifteen-year-olds, we talked to hundreds of parents, educators, and young adolescents. We chatted with many more over the electronic highway. Over and over again the theme of privacy emerged as did the controversial debate over teens' rights to it and parents' responsibility surrounding it. Over the Internet we counseled mothers and fathers, stepparents and grandparents, sketching fair boundaries with regard to a child's private life. We debated the fine points of what to do (or not to do) with information a parent retrieved by the stealth of reading a diary or sneaking into a bedroom.

After realizing over time how pervasive the dilemma of privacy is, and how much anxiety surrounded privacy—its right and its violation—we decided to spend time conducting focus groups. In public and private schools in different parts of the country, we conducted interviews with young adolescents on this sensitive topic. We were eager to hear their views and understand their grievances. In addition to that person-to-person investigation, we designed three questionnaires: one for parents; one for educators including administrators, counselors, and teachers; and one for middle school students. These generated feedback on a variety of questions pertaining to middlers' tendency for holding back information and even lying, as well as the issue of privacy.

Coincidentally as we write our book, privacy is perhaps the number one debate throughout America. In every corner of our culture, arguments are raging over individual rights versus security and privacy. Cyberspace is hotly contested. Free speech on the electronic highway is staunchly defended by some, yet challenged by others who insist the protection of juveniles from Internet predators or conniving marketeers is paramount. Celebrities smeared in tabloids or photographed sunbathing topless in their own backyards sue for invasion of privacy, pushing the envelope on how much they owe their fans. Movies like *Minority Report* tackle the privacy issue underneath high-tech plot lines.

Schools have become battlegrounds, too. Is it a service to post exam results on bulletin boards and Web sites, or a blatant violation of a student's privacy? The Supreme Court's agenda includes an Oklahoma lawsuit filed by a mother claiming that her son's experience of having his grades shouted out in class violated his Fourteenth Amendment rights and a federal statute designed to protect the confidentiality of his academic record.

Before the 9/11 terror attacks, debates wrangled over wiretaps and searches, but since, these arguments have reached fever proportions. The CIA, FBI, and INS (Immigration and Naturalization Service) claim that more invasive measures—tapping all our communications, for example—are absolutely necessary, justified in order to protect Americans. Homeland security strategists envision an operation called TIPS wherein mail carriers and UPS drivers do double duty as tipsters. In communities across America, newspaper columnists and cable pundits wonder out loud, is Operation TIPS vigilance or vigilantism? What's next? Neighbors tattling on each other, kids snitching on older brothers and sisters, or on elders as Nazi youth did? Every branch of government—the legislative, judicial, and executive—talks about the Constitution more than anyone has since the days of the founding fathers.

These are serious times all right. Danger has invaded our own backyards. Current events do feature privacy breaches and the fact that people are not objecting to such invasions of privacy as they may have two years ago! And yet, the bounds of privacy—how much is appropriate—and the fairness of breaching, is a topic that parents and their adolescents have *always* debated.

Perhaps the stakes are higher now. When we wrote *The Roller-Coaster Years*, our first parenting book back in 1997, we commiserated with mothers, fathers, and stepparents about the darker world in which today's children come of age. As teens, neither we, nor our parents, had to guard against Internet perverts. Nor did we have to fear a kiss could be a fast track to AIDS. Back in those days, an M&M was merely a color-coated chocolate candy, not a controversial rap artist (Eminem). *Ecstasy* described a state of mind, not the popular designer drug that threatens youth en masse. *Hooking up* referred to telephone lines, not casual oral sex on Friday night. The phenomenon of "the school shooting" didn't erupt every spring. And a cell referred to a biology definition of matter, not a coven of terrorists plotting mayhem in a condominium around the block.

With so many heart-stopping potential scenarios surrounding our children, many parents feel pressured to trounce on trust. Allowing a child privacy is simply too risky.

Furthermore, adults are on the receiving end of a chorus warning, "Stay involved." Yes, countless experts wag their fingers at parents, insisting that ignorance is not bliss when it comes to adolescents. Teenagers are getting into mischief, getting high, plotting revenge, and sleeping around. You have to know exactly what's happening in the lives of your sons and daughters lest you become the next clueless parent in an endless parade of headline stories like these:

- Eighth-grader Charles Bishop crashes a four-seat Cessna airplane into a forty-two story Tampa building leaving behind a handwritten note explaining that his suicide mission intended to show his support for Osama bin Laden. The fifteen-year-old's fate dumbfounded classmates, neighbors, teachers, and his mother. Patriotic, polite, an honor student with all A's on his December report card, a flag bearer belting out *The Star Spangled Banner*, a kid who washed airplanes to finance flying lessons— none of these descriptions belied a kamikaze-esque lunatic. January 7, 2002.

- Boy, eleven, arrested for placing four threats including "School shooting tomorrow," "Kill Mr. Collins," and "bombing today" on top of the urinal in the boys' bathroom at the Harry B. Thompson Middle School in Syosset, New York. The boy was considered a good student in the school and had no prior disciplinary problems. No one had any inkling of why this boy behaved like this. Crying and remorseful, he was released into the custody of his parents. May 2, 2001.

- Fifteen-year-old from Wrentham, Massachusetts, a suburb of Boston, was kidnapped and sexually tortured, and beaten by three sadomasochistic adults with whom she rendezvoused at a mall after meeting them on the Internet. In her stunned mother's company, she told the FBI all the details of her abduction. August 2001.

- Thirteen-year-old seventh-grader Nathaniel Brazill, after being sent home from Lake Worth Community Middle School on the last day of classes for throwing water balloons, returned to school with a semi-automatic Raven pistol and fatally shot a teacher in the face. His grandmother said, "I thought he was the best boy." The school board spokesman described the boy as earning A's and B's and having perfect attendance, and "no problems of any kind prior to this." May 26, 2000.

It's impossible to imagine the state of mind of parents who discover their "good kid" is a suicide, a rape victim who cavorts secretly on the Net, or a felon. These stories are so unbelievable and their stars so ordinary that the result is no parent feels immune. Too many of us shudder over the supporting cast of mothers, fathers, and grandparents. It could be anyone.

Wary, parents scout, prod, and even pilfer information about their young adolescents. Some turn to technology or software enabling a sneak peek. A few go to outlandish extremes like a Voorhees, New Jersey, councilman who subjected his teenage daughters to a saliva swab as they returned home from a party to check for drinking.

Needless to say, actions like these put adults and their adolescents at loggerheads. The stakes, namely the safety of your precious child, are high. The temptation to resort to KGB-like tactics may surface. Keep in mind that most young adolescents are *not* stockpiling weapons in their bedroom closets. Most are *not* selling drugs from their backpacks. Most are *not* conspiring with kooks on-line.

The reality is that our young adolescents are trying to survive the rites and rigors of adolescence. Our sons and our daughters are grappling with coming-of-age questions. Where do I fit in? Am I normal? They are attempting to maneuver through the adventures and the risks that every other generation before them faced, too. The temptation to get into a car with a friend who has a beer in his hand, the question of whether or not to participate in a stupid prank, the urge to experiment sexually—teenagers since the beginning of time have had the same instincts.

Ten- to fifteen-year-olds, especially, rather than being up to no good, are more often simply embarrassed when their parents know too much about their foibles and failures. Their agenda is more likely test anxiety about that biology quiz or stress because they are having a bad hair day or sporting a big fat blemish on one cheek.

The challenge is for parents to find out what's really happening in the lives of their offspring. However, first calm down. Most of the adolescent population is not destined for terror or plotting secret lives. Choosing a parenting style that smacks of constant surveillance is overreacting. Gestapo and guerrilla tactics sabotage close parent-child relationships and pollute family dynamics. An adolescent who is under a microscope is more apt to clam up and shut you out at a time when he or she needs you the most.

This book intends to show parents how to keep themselves well informed about their child's world and state of mind without invading a child's privacy or stifling a child. Our aim is to identify and explore six privacy zones in a chapter for each:

1. The Bedroom. What goes on inside is worthy of investigation, but not for the reasons most parents think. The bedroom is more than a messy battle zone.
2. The Body. Between the years of ten and fifteen, a boy's body and a girl's body develop dramatically. Those days of sponge-bathing baby and dwelling on every bump and change are long gone. Parents can't peek but need to be aware of what's happening within those developing bodies.
3. Friends. The good, the bad, and the dangerous se-

cret societies are analyzed. You can't pick your
young adolescent's friends, but you can learn to
pick up on warning signs.

4. The Internet. Young adolescents take fingers to
keyboard to reveal heartfelt emotions. They take
advantage of the panoply of communication devices at their disposal—computers, cell phones,
regular phones, and hand-held electronic organiz-
ers that can send text messages. Parents are
tempted to wiretap without obtaining a search war-
rant, but this invasion may be counterproductive

5. Romance and Sexuality. Not every romantic encounter is a dangerous liaison, but parents must assist a child as she navigates love and lust (without
sneaking into the cineplex and sitting in the back
row to clandestinely chaperone).

6. School. The same parents who reviewed homework
in grade school are stunned when their child refuses to share school stuff during middle school.
How much do you need to know? Can learning too
much sabotage your child's learning?

You will see how to satisfy your need to know while respecting
your ten- to fifteen-year-old's parallel need to grow independently. We will show you how to move around your daughter's
personal territory, your son's turf. Where is a parent's presence
most needed? We answer that question as we weigh confidentiality. Within each privacy zone, we will educate parents about
typical adolescent cover-ups. We will carve out the latitudes to

leave alone to your child, those taboo invasions. Finally, we dissect information overload because sometimes too much knowledge can be a bad thing.

As a society we are very sensitive—and becoming more so each day—with regard to protecting our precious privacy. Caroline Kennedy Schlossberg's classic book, coauthored with Ellen Alderman, *The Right to Privacy*, sounded a warning gong: an individual's life is no longer private. Big Brother is indeed watching. The coauthors say, "You ask anyone and they will tell you that they have a fundamental right to privacy. The right to privacy is what makes us civilized."

When we as a society blast big government, corporations, tabloids, and telemarketers for invasions of privacy, we cannot afford to sanction what is no less than "a double standard of privacy" with regard to our relationship with our young adolescents. There is something wrong with steamrolling over a child's personal sanctuary and private life. While there is no exact age to sanction total privacy, no clear-cut cutoff point when questions are inappropriate, privacy and respect should evolve as children grow into young adulthood.

Our book advocates that parents define and outline a family privacy policy. As you read what to do and what not to do, the fine lines and blurred ones will become clearer. The closer you get to your child and to the thoughts he or she holds close, the less you will think about underhandedly hunting for the truth. You will learn what lies behind your son's stare or your daughter's smile.

We intend to help you use reason to guide you. Furthermore, we encourage you and show you how to cultivate your wisdom and follow your heart. When you reject the urge to crack open a lock or a password, you become more successful at cracking the mysterious code that fragile young adolescents construct to hide their worries and wonders. The more you value and respect your child's precious privacy, the more value your son or your daughter will place on your relationship. You can build a bond where secrets between you, and throughout your family, are rare.

As a starting point, we offer the following test:

Do You **Really** Know Your Child?

You catch your daughter in a lie. It turns out she wasn't where she said she would be. Or you discover your son did something you never thought he'd do. It gives you pause. Uh-oh.

Can any young adolescent be trusted? Can yours? Take this quiz to see how well you really know your child—his or her fears, friends, and potential foibles.

Directions: Choose only one answer.

1. When was the last time your child confided a secret about a friend—a secret the parents of that teen would find disconcerting?

a) When it comes to my teen's friends, mum's the word.
b) I confess that I haven't spent much time talking with my teenager lately.
c) Recently I learned something really troubling.

2. My teenager's most pressing worry is

a) the upcoming midterm or getting a date for the social.
b) getting grounded.
c) I'll have to think about that one because I'm not sure what's on my teen's mind these days.

3. Where does your behavior fall on the to-snoop-or-not-to-snoop debate?

a) If I had a suspicion, I'd go through my teen's backpack and drawers.
b) I do not snoop because I think every child's privacy should be respected.
c) I rifle through my teen's room regularly, looking in drawers, reading notes, and checking the backpack.

4. Can you name your teenager's favorite pop, rap, or rock star?

a) Yes, I know whom my teen idolizes.
b) My parents never listened to my music when I was a teenager and now I know why, because I can't bear listening to my teen's choices.
c) I'd like to know the answer to that but my child listens silently with headphones as a rule.

5. In your opinion can any adolescent be trusted?

a) No, their hormones program them to take dangerous risks and have dangerous liaisons.
b) Absolutely; being trustworthy and making mistakes are two different issues and teens are capable of both.
c) Most of the time, but not always.

6. What does your teenager do during study hall?

a) Good question and I am afraid to know the answer.
b) I don't know, study I guess.
c) Different things—sometimes study for a test, sometimes homework, and other times just read a new fan magazine or a book.

7. Can you name the R-rated movies your teenager has watched in the last few weeks?

a) Yes. I have allowed my teen to see a few after previewing them and deciding they were okay.
b) That is impossible because TV is filled with last year's R-rated fare and I can't keep up with all the trash at the local cinema.
c) I keep an eye out here at home but I don't know what my teen watches at friends' homes.

8. Some teenagers, namely girls, have been known to dress one way so they can get out the door, and then change into edgier, sexier clothes and makeup before entering the party. Is your daughter one of these?

a) I don't think so but what with sleepovers and such I don't always see what my child looks like.
b) No, I do the laundry and I know her clothes.
c) Could be, because we've had fights about skimpy tops, tight pants, and overdone makeup.

9. Your teen comes home from a party and you smell cigarette smoke on her clothing. Do you

a) assume nothing, because cigarette smoke clings to anyone who walks through it.
b) know in your gut your child is smoking cigarettes even though you asked before and she denied doing so.
c) make a mental note to ask about the smoking habits of her friends.

10. Do you know if your child receives a school detention, a late slip, or a notice to retake a test?

a) No.
b) Yes.
c) I think so, unless he hides the information from me.

11. Guesstimate how much sexual experience your teenager has had.

a) I can't deal with this.
b) I've spoken to my teen about first base, second base, third base, and I think she's still running the bases but hasn't gone for the home run.
c) I have tried to talk about sex but my teenager says "I can't talk about that stuff."

12. Are you familiar with the peer, teacher, or adult your child admires most?

a) Yes, my teen has shared his admiration with me.
b) I am not aware that he admires anyone in particular.
c) Now you have really tweaked my curiosity—I'd like to know the answer to that.

13. You hear there is a fight in the parking lot at school involving several students. Do you

a) get a sick feeling because you just know your child is one of the culprits.

b) make a few calls to find out who the culprits are, to satisfy your curiosity.

c) file the incident away because you know it is not your child and no immediate concern of yours.

14. How has your adolescent felt about the rash of school shootings?

a) My teenager is distressed and has identified troubled kids at school.

b) I have not heard my teen comment nor have I.

c) My adolescent doesn't often share his thoughts with me on anything but I imagine he is nervous.

Scoring

1.	a) 5	b) 10	c) 15
2.	a) 15	b) 5	c) 10
3.	a) 10	b) 15	c) 5
4.	a) 15	b) 5	c) 10
5.	a) 5	b) 15	c) 10
6.	a) 5	b) 10	c) 15
7.	a) 15	b) 5	c) 10
8.	a) 10	b) 15	c) 5
9.	a) 15	b) 5	c) 10
10.	a) 5	b) 15	c) 10
11.	a) 5	b) 15	c) 10
12.	a) 15	b) 5	c) 10
13.	a) 5	b) 10	c) 15
14.	a) 15	b) 5	c) 10

0-75 Points—A Stranger in Your House

If you scored in this range, you do not know your young adolescent very well. Your relationship falls short in the intimacy department. It looks as if you and your child are not into trading confidential information. Nor are you and your child in sync most of the time about the details and happenings of daily life. In all likelihood your life is so busy that you have dropped the ball about what's going on with your child. Add to that a middler's natural reluctance to share secrets (or detention slips) with a parent. What you have is family members leading separate lives. This is not good. You need to have more than suspicions and worry where your son or daughter is concerned. The best way to get to know a child is to listen to music together, review movies (maybe even an R-rated one), and talk about friends and issues that are on a child's mind. Your child needs you more than you think right now and more than you know.

80-145 Points—A Mystery in Your House

If you scored in this range, your young adolescent is like a mystery. The questions tickled your curiosity about your child and raised some interesting issues, but you are too often clueless or uncertain when it comes to what's going on in the mind of your child. Chances are that you have tried to get closer or talk to your child but have been rebuffed. Young adolescents crave a private life and do tend to shut parents out from time to time. And yet, you have to find a better strategy for getting inside the head of your own child. Don't give up so easily and don't settle for not knowing the answers to the questions that are on your mind. Why? Because the things you worry about are on your teen's mind, too, even if it's hard to trade information. Spend more time with your teen.

150-210—No Stranger, No Mystery in Your House

If you scored here, give yourself a big pat on the back. Young adolescents are not the easiest folks to get close to—and you have done it. Children this age tend not to be particularly open. Furthermore, many clam up when parents try to discuss sensitive issues. You do not worry about your child because you know what is on her mind, on her plate from day to day, and who is in her thoughts. The more a parent and a middler can exchange confidences and the small details of everyday life, the closer the bond. This gives parents the opportunity to inject their values and gives a son or a daughter the opportunity to feel connected and loved. Keep up the good work.

Chapter 1

The Bedroom

"Knock three times before you enter."

My bedroom is on the third floor.
My mother broke her kneecap,
so now she can't come up.

—Seventh-grade girl

ave you noticed this yet? One day your daughter is content sitting at the kitchen table doing schoolwork under your wing. Or your son parks himself nightly next to you, watching TV till bedtime. Then seemingly overnight, you notice your child is gone. Your son no longer shadows you. Your daughter spends nearly all free time in her bedroom. As children grow into adolescents, boys and girls gravitate away from family areas such as the den, living room, or finished basement and move into their bedrooms.

This change of routine is perfectly natural and normal. Parents, not middlers, often have a hard time adjusting. Human nature being what it is, many mothers' and fathers' knee-jerk reaction is to become suspect. A parent begins to ask: What are you doing in there? *What's going on in there?* Underneath is concern that something bad might be happening behind that closed door.

In our first book, *The Roller-Coaster Years: Raising Your Child Through the Maddening Yet Magical Middle School Years*, we prided ourselves on alerting parents to developmental milestones that ten- to fifteen-year-olds (as we coined this age group "middlers") experience. A major turning point is the emerging need for privacy. Around age twelve, children begin to think of themselves as having their own lives, apart from family. They hold their thoughts, feelings, and their relationships closer to their hearts. The child who once seemed to be an open book now closes the covers. As your child moves through early and into later adolescence, she is likely to share less information with you. You may even get the feeling that she is becoming downright secretive.

Keep in mind, though, that middlers grow at different rates. Some barely ten-year-olds bristle at every question you pose or comment you offer. "My parents try to give me a speech about *everything*," huffs a twelve-year-old boy from New Hampshire in our survey. And yet other fourteen-year-olds may still be telling you every detail about their daily lives without a prompt. Whether your child is nine or thirteen is irrelevant, though, because you will know when that need for privacy begins. How?

He will be spending more and more time away from you either with peers or hanging out in his room. Don't panic.

In this chapter, we'll tell you how to get inside your child's head, and inside his room, without having to resort to undercover tactics. Rather than seeing a child's room as a hostile bunker begging for a break-and-enter offensive, we will advise you how to make it over into a discovery zone. Therein lies information, evidence, and secrets. Our guidelines will show you how to effortlessly gather all the information you need in order to feel comfortable.

Getting to Know Your Way Around— Their Bedroom

As children move into double digits—ten, eleven, twelve— they covet control over their comings and goings. They seek independence. The bedroom becomes personal territory. Once upon a time, only a parent closed a child's door so a little one could nap without the disturbing noises of the family. During these years, it's your child who will be closing the door. A new knock etiquette comes into play. Entering without knocking is defined as "barging in." Even if your child isn't putting a Do Not Disturb sign on the doorknob, you get the sense that you are not always welcome.

The changing of the guard at the bedroom door signals change. Your child is staking her claim for ownership over her bedroom. She wants you to observe her idea of the protocol. Protocol? Many of us aren't even aware of how we do enter our child's domain, much less that sensitivity is in order.

In our survey we ask ten- to fifteen-year-olds, "If your mother or father wanted to come into your room, how would they act?" Half (50 percent) reported their parents would come in *without* knocking. Mothers and fathers rated themselves far more considerate than their offspring rated them. Next time, knock.

When you do go into that room during these years, you will notice changes. The bedroom fills up with clutter. As children morph into adolescents, music scores the transition, loudly or silently inside headphones. Like all good parents, you want to get into this privacy zone because it is the latitude and longitude of what's happening inside your child. If you are like the majority, you make a huge mistake. You try to fight your way in.

Sidestep the Messy War Zone

Over the years, we quizzed parents to reflect on the biggest battleground they had faced with their adolescents. We offered a list of scenarios. Back talk? Unsavory friends? Drugs and alcohol? Messy room? The majority of parents confessed their child's messy room created the most fireworks.

The bedroom does indeed have the potential to become the universal battleground. The typical parental battle cry is "Clean that room." The usual retort is "It's MY room!" Or "Leave me alone." The operative words here are *my* and *me*. The right to be a packrat and live in a pigsty is vigorously defended. In the battle for independence that adolescents wage, control over the state of the bedroom is the prize.

Initially, the messy room controversy surprised us. In a

world with the specter of AIDS and Ecstasy hovering, populated by tattooed punks and wild-childs with pierced bellybuttons and peeking thongs, where fresh-mouthed kids verbalize disrespect, why did unmade beds or strewn wrinkled clothing unhinge mothers and fathers so?

After searching the souls of parents and interviewing experts on early adolescence, we learned the messy room conflict is not really about dirty socks or discarded sweatshirts. It's deeper. It is about authority and discipline. When a child retreats into her own world and takes a stand, it feels threatening to a parent in the authority department. Some parents turn downright reactionary, resorting to I'm-the-boss mode, a recipe for instant and repeated argument. It's as if we fear if we give an inch, our children will steal a yard.

Avoid this trap. Take a deep breath here. Don't think *pigsty* or *packrat* even if those terms are on the tip of your tongue every time you glance into your child's doorway. If you see only disarray you are missing a more important perspective. If you remain bent on establishing your dictatorial order, you deny yourself a golden opportunity.

Think and Act like an Anthropologist

In the world of espionage, there is a term, *humint*. It stands for human intelligence, all the information that comes voluntarily from individuals versus data that is unearthed by devious means such as bugging phone lines or hacking into computers. *Humint* is a term and a tactic you can master.

Instead of focusing on discipline, we suggest you choose,

literally, the discipline of anthropology. Why? Your child's room is actually a treasure trove, albeit a disorganized and disheveled one. Think of it as an archaeological dig. Greet it with curiosity. Treat all the contents therein with delicacy and respect. Okay, we can see visions of smelly Skechers and crumpled brown khakis dancing across your increasingly doubtful mind, but wait. The contents for better or worse hold the clues to who your child is, and is becoming. Anything (and everything) that intrigues or bores him exists within those four walls. They contain yesterday's cherished memories and tomorrow's dreams.

Take an inventory. There's the stuff of childhood. This may include Star War Legos or Barbies, action figures, board games, or baseball cards. Then there's the stuff pointing toward adolescence: cologne, bodybuilding or fan magazines, makeup, CD players, CDs that you swear are breeding. There may be assorted remnants of hobbies such as a musical instrument gathering dust, a microscope or telescope, ballet shoes, a mineral-collecting kit, or an ant farm. Add evidence of sports like cleats, hockey sticks, tennis rackets. Books, backpack, handheld Gameboys—you get the picture. No wonder there is no room to move, much less an easy way to arrange all this stuff.

Examine the walls. Do you see photographs, autographs, movie stubs, or concert backstage-pass decals?

The clean-freak gene in you wants to weed through all this, throw out childhood toys, discard the used soda cup from the hockey game or concert. Wait a minute. Could any of these hold sentimental value? Most do. Each says something of significance *to* your child and *about* him. If you fail to see the meaning of the artifacts, you are being insensitive to your child.

Realize your son or daughter still values the child within. These years are "in between" ones. Your child moves back and forth between childhood and adolescence with ambivalence from week to week, day to day, even hour to hour. You see this when your thirteen-year-old sucks on a lollipop while doing a complicated algebra equation. Your son squirms in front of a cartoon video game one minute, then the next minute wants you to take him to buy supplements so he can bulk up so as to be more attractive to girls. Most young adolescents are reluctant to let go of that childish self even as they race headlong into acting grown up. Let him decide when to cast aside the remnants of childhood.

Express interest in items around the room. Ask, "Why are you saving this movie stub?" Or "I see that you saved this soccer patch, wasn't that a great game!" Point to your child's CDs and inquire who his favorite artist is. Reminisce about which album you couldn't wait to buy at the record store even if she rolls her eyes as you mention Barry Manilow or David Cassidy. Or worse, if she dates you with a quip like "Paul McCartney, wasn't he in *Wings*?"

Ask her to play you her latest CD. Studies done on young adolescents show that listening to music is a solitary activity for most kids. If you can't understand the lyrics, ask to see the CD jacket. Music is the window to the soul of adolescents—always was and always will be. If this leads to debate, share opinions and, above all, listen.

Arrange a Room Within a Room

When a testy preteen, paranoid about her privacy to begin with, has to share a bedroom, the conflict heats up.

"It's not my parents driving me crazy, it's my brother," seethed an eleven-year-old boy in one of our focus groups. His frustration-edged remark unleashed a firestorm of similar complaints from the others sitting cross-legged in a circle. Oh, how they counted the sibling invasions: "helping herself to my CDs," and "stealing my clothes out of my closet and using my makeup"; "teasing comments," "reading my e-mails."

One thirteen-year-old we talked to complained about a situation *even worse*. "How'd you like to share your bedroom with a stranger?" That's exactly what happens when families blend. A teen finds himself bunking with a stepbrother or a stepsister. Add loyalty conflicts, jealousy, and annoyance over being shuttled between households.

Sibling snafus are everyday experiences in families and stepfamilies with children close in age. Moving to a bigger house where each child gets a bedroom isn't realistic for most families. Short of that, though, there are things a parent can do.

Acknowledge your child's desire for privacy. See things from her perspective. Younger children are pesky, at least some of the time. Take her aside and ask her to tell you what behaviors irk her the most. You can't exile a brother or sister to the cellar or attic, but you can create boundaries in their behavior department. "Don't take your sister's stuff without asking permission." After that powwow, take aside the younger child and explain what is off-limits, whether it's the CD collection or something else. Both parties need to be handled with finesse. A younger child feeling rejected benefits from your explaining why his older brother or sister suddenly finds him "repugnant." The preteen relishes being treated more grown up and having you act on his behalf.

Discuss territorial claims. Stepfamilies and blended families require sensitivity. Territorial battles are common. While easy solutions rarely exist, patience and commiseration can go a long way to making all young adolescent and younger parties feel better.

Allow a young adolescent time alone in her bedroom at least some of the time. When she has friends over, keep the younger ones occupied elsewhere.

Design the layout of the shared bedroom to allot each child space. Divvy up the closet or the bureau drawers. Hang shelving for each.

Empower Your Child to Create a Sanctuary

If it's occurred to you that the Mickey Mouse decals in your middlers' room no longer suit them, you are not alone. They've outgrown Noah's Ark, cartoon characters, unicorns, or fairy-tale bed sheets. First time around, designing the bedroom space fell into your domain. This time give the revamping job to your children. Shelve your ideas; rely on their ideas instead.

A bedroom should be akin to an artist's canvas: expressive, comforting, and stimulating.

Expressive: One of the main questions with which young adolescents grapple is "Who am I?" The tween years is the time for kids to figure out the answer. The toys, books, wall hangings, calendars, music, mysterious minutiae, and other stuff chosen are all pieces to this puzzle. They define identity. Experts insist that's why ten- to fifteen-year-olds become collectors in the first place. They amass and experiment in the quest to establish a self. One year it's wrestling for him or field hockey for her; next year those are passé. Boys and girls dress as jocks or preppies, skateboarders or freaks to define their social memberships. They move in and out of persons, as they search for one that feels right.

Watching a child dive into a passion for the saxophone, and then never want to practice (after you've paid dearly for the rental or purchase of said instrument) is annoying. You may even feel as if you've raised a quitter. Keep in mind that a short attention span to certain things—activities, hobbies, interests—is typical. What counts is encouraging a child to explore. These are the years when skills develop. Middle schools characteristically offer many clubs and after-school activities because they want to give middlers opportunities to try out as many things as possible—chorus, photography, theater, sports, volunteerism, and so forth. At home your job is to continue the theme of exploration.

Your child's room should be his own individual petri dish where he dabbles in as much as possible. Think of it as his cocoon.

Comforting: Did your child once cuddle a special blanket? Researchers at the University of Wisconsin verified that children's special blankets had the same magical powers as Mommy during doctor visits. After studying sixty-four children, they found that blankets known to be attached emotionally to the boys and girls in the experiment appeared to lessen their anxiety in the doctor's office as much as a mother's presence. "Blankies" are magic.

Your children may outgrow blankie. What remains is the equation that certain items contribute to a sense of security. These years are filled with change, turbulence, and insecurity. So being surrounded by favorite things is reassuring and especially important now. Your role is to guide your young adolescent to create a room for relaxing.

A comfy bed is a must for middlers, who need an increasing amount of sleep. Well-worn stuffed animals, special collections—whatever things your child holds figuratively if not literally on to are objects of comfort. The room is supposed to be a sanctuary.

Order is not necessarily a part of this atmosphere. As we already mentioned, neatness is a herculean task for ten- to fifteen-year-olds. Neatnik does not come naturally to most middlers. Spend a weekend putting up shelving or a closet organizing kit. Keeping the room clean has to be explained in specifics. No food items left around. Dirty clothes put in the laundry hamper. Floors or rugs vacuumed on a regular basis. When you talk in specifics, your child has a better chance of understanding the directions—and following them.

Stimulating: Young adolescent bedrooms should be a place

for adventure and activity, for studying and learning. That doesn't mean we advocate furnishing it with TV, VCR, Play Station, PC, telephone, and any other electronic innovation your child covets. Without her own personal television or DVD, she's more likely to watch programs or movies with you. If you provide her with everything in her own space, she's less likely to join the family.

So much has been written about the hectic schedules our children have today. An unrecognized yet critical part of being stimulated is actually "vegging out." We forget that ten- to fifteen-year-olds desperately need time and space simply *to be*. Middlers are dealing with physical, emotional, psychological, and social changes pulsing through their lives.

If you see your child staring at the ceiling, realize that this is a useful and necessary time-out. Don't jump to the conclusion he is slothful or she must be stoned. Zoning out is leading to something, perhaps to something even extraordinary. Did you know that Albert Einstein discovered his theory of relativity while sprawled out on a hill basking in a summer day? He did not make this intellectual leap from behind his desk. So if your child is horizontal, don't think idle. Think incubating. The room is supposed to be a kind of percolator.

Treating your child's space with respect, curiosity, and patience comes with a guarantee. That Do Not Disturb sign, actual or implied, will be replaced (at least occasionally) with a Welcome sign. Your child will invite you in to show you something or play you a new CD track. When you abandon the clean machine mentality and approach, you will find a truce, and even better—camaraderie.

Cover-ups—
To Worry or Not to Worry

Most of what goes on in your middler's bedroom as you read these pages is what has gone on for decades. Talking with friends (although telephones are now being exchanged for cell phones), daydreaming, listening to music, and writing in diaries. Young adolescents need their own space and their own place to let down their defenses without being judged by an adult.

However, there are signs that may make you worry.

Hostility: While few adolescents will have the gall to affix a lock to their bedroom door, watch for behaviors that spell unusual trouble. Is your child's room totally off-limits? A posted KEEP OUT message is little cause for concern, unless it is followed up regularly by fights when you step inside to drop off laundry. When your child takes this combative posture about his room, you are likely to know too little about what's going on with him.

Isolation: Another pattern to watch out for is hyper-hibernating. Is your child alone in his room all the time, even on weekends? Some children are loners. A solitary six-year-old may be comfortable with this temperament, but ten- to fifteen-year-olds need peers. It is true that not all young adolescents have a pack mentality, surrounding themselves constantly with friends, but nearly every middler has at least one or two friends. If your child is friendless, never gets phone calls, or rarely plays with other children, find out why.

Typically, middlers run into social problems at school with cliques and bullying. Social conflicts feel like shameful failures. So if you sense your child is hiding or brooding, investigate further at school.

Weirdness: What if your child's room decor looks as if Ozzy Osbourne or Marilyn Manson did the interior—satanistic posters, a CD rack filled with suicide rock like Kurt Cobain, bookshelves of Sylvia Plath, black walls. That's what the following parent faced:

"My fifteen-year-old daughter dresses in black and wears leather necklaces and black nail polish. The posters on her wall scare me. She listens to Stevie Nicks all the time and reads books about witches. Is this unhealthy? I have heard it described as Gothic. Is she in need of therapy?"

Chances are New Age paperbacks about witches, heavy metal music, gruesome paraphernalia, and Goth clothes are sheer experimentation. Young adolescents like to try on identities as they search for who they are becoming.

Too much weirdness sets off the parental alarm bell. Automatically we think Columbine's trenchcoat mafia. An outlandish or disturbing personal style may be signaling emotional distress. Anger and depression hit some young adolescents hard. If your young adolescent's style unnerves you, use this checklist to get a clearer picture.

- Is she well adjusted in school, working up to her potential?
- Does she have friends with whom she laughs and spends time?
- Does she have interests and habits that seem typical, such as watching *TRL* (MTV's *Total Request Live*) or meeting her friends at the mall for pizza?

- Does she talk to you about how she is feeling about her life?
- Does she participate willingly in family routines?

If you answer *yes* enough, don't worry. If you answer *no, no, no,* make an appointment with the social worker or psychologist at your child's school. Inquire about teen screening. The Youth Depression Screening Initiative offers a test nationwide wherein kids hear questions through headphones and type responses on a laptop computer, ensuring privacy. The Center for the Advancement of Children's Mental Health at Columbia University works with schools and communities to administer the test and any follow-up treatment. (Contact www.kidsmentalhealth.org.)

Adolescent depression, anxiety, and suicide are widespread enough so parents shouldn't dismiss the signs as legendary teen angst. Surveys conducted by the U.S. Centers for Disease Control and Prevention reveal that 20 percent of teenagers say they have thought about ending their life.

For most of us, though, our young adolescents are not holing up in a dangerous state of mind nor hiding out in deranged environments. That said, make no mistake; many are standing their ground.

Taboo Invasions of a Child's Sacred Spaces

Over 2001's Thanksgiving weekend in a coastal Massachusetts town south of Boston, two fifteen-year-old boys and the older brother (age seventeen) of one were taken from their bedrooms to the police station, charged with plotting school violence intended to be *bloodier* than the 1999 Columbine, Colorado, massacre. Summonses went out to other apparent confidants— a fifteen-year-old boy and a seventeen-year-old girl suspected of having knowledge of this dastardly plot.

According to investigators, the intended scenario boasted bombs, guns, a massacre of teachers and students, and a climactic suicide on the school's roof. Evidence ranged from an overheard threat turned in by a student, to a landlord's tip-off of a suspicious box nearby that contained part of a bomb, to a note found by the custodian in the school hallway alluding to the attack. A search of the boys' bedrooms yielded shotgun shells, knives, a notebook with bomb-making instructions, and photographs of the boys brandishing guns. Closed case? Hardly.

The parents, despite the blatant evidence, tried to convince authorities that the boys were not really dangerous. They conceded the boys were troubled and insisted it was understandable. Circumstances such as a father's recent death, divorce, and ADD that stymied academic progress were cited to explain what they insisted was dabbling in pretend mischief. They cast the ammunition and photos as souvenirs from a family vacation in Ohio. Since the boys were stopped short, it remains unclear how far they would have gone. The parents, however, would never admit their kids were headed for the annals of catastrophe.

After the Columbine tragedy, the Colorado town's sheriff lamented that it wouldn't have happened if every parent searched through every child's room. Yet as this incident proves, a search isn't always telling to a parent. Finding suspicious stuff isn't always enough. Reading notebooks, scouring bureau drawers, rifling through closets isn't always conclusive. It takes more than snooping to really get inside a young adolescent's mind and intentions. You have to really know who your son is, what your daughter is thinking.

The following tactics are becoming widespread, according to our survey of parents. However, they are not foolproof.

A room search: If you are looking for justification to search through your child's bureau drawers, closet, or desk, you will find it. There are those who insist a clandestine shortcut is justified and effective. Be forewarned, because middlers can sense when you've been snooping. "I know my mother snooped in my room because my stuff was moved. I could tell," reports a twelve-year-old New Hampshire girl. How did she know? Young adolescents have a sixth sense here because their room is their castle. It's their business and they keep a diligent watch over their domain.

A parent reasons: *What better way to know if my child is experimenting with drugs, smoking cigarettes, than to scour for drug paraphernalia, rolling papers, or any suspicious-looking contraband?* If a mother worries: *Is my son's anger dangerous to himself or others? How best to ease my mind than to check a bedroom just to make sure there are no shotgun shells mixed in with his underwear?* A parent is on guard: *If I have doubts about the influence of rock or rap, why not take a sneak listen to his CD collection?*

Consider this, though. If you find marijuana and go charging after your young adolescent, he will focus angrily on your invading his privacy. The issue becomes very quickly and heatedly your violation of privacy. Meanwhile he sidesteps the charges and denies the truth of your find. Is that progress?

Reading a diary: This is the ultimate betrayal. You are not just rifling through material things but stealing right into the soul of your child. Many parents admit to this personal violation. They rationalize: *I wanted to find out why my daughter is so sad or if she's being teased at school.* Or a parent feels detective work is in order: *I am fearful my child is having oral sex and the diary will prove yea or nay.*

In the final analysis, do you have the right or even the responsibility to invade your child's personal space and property? Should you? Only you as the parent can ultimately decide if you have sufficient and rightful grounds. But before you snoop, draw this equation for yourself. What will you gain? Knowledge. Although, let us remind you, not necessarily peace of mind. What will you lose? Trust and intimacy.

The "HOW DARE YOU" will cost you dearly in the long term. Only in the most serious scenarios should you take this search-and-seizure strategy. Why? Your child will not confide or confess the secrets of her private life—much less ask your opinion on private matters—if you take the sneaky barge-and-enter route. Instead she will retreat, withhold, lie, and close the door more firmly not only to her room but to her heart.

Forfeiting a rapport with your child is the worst thing you can do. Every year the Virginia-based nonprofit Horatio Alger Association gauges adolescent attitudes and releases a report called "State of Our Nation's Youth." In 2001, 84 percent of the teenagers polled said their future success will be defined by whether they have close family relationships. You hold the key to the quality of the rapport you develop with your child.

Rather than peeking or pilfering where you don't belong, here is a more productive way to retrieve valuable insights into your child. To get more information by taking the high road, have your child add to that canvass.

Hang a bulletin board in your middler's bedroom. You can purchase one inexpensively. Or you can turn it into a family project. You can go to the hardware store and get some corkboard. Martha Stewart recommends covering it with fabric and crisscrossing it with ribbon to make inserting photographs and papers neat and convenient. (Beware: This finicky recipe may turn you on in direct proportion to turning off your middler.) You can also take an old picture frame, add backing, and glue on old corks. Whichever type of bulletin board you encourage or supply, each one becomes a revealing backdrop.

"My daughter's bulletin board is a potpourri of what she loves—newspaper clippings on her favorite hockey players, concert ticket stubs from concerts she has attended, cartoons poking fun at her shortcomings, key chains from friends, patches from rival soccer teams, pictures of cute boys, and other mementos."

Do you see how much information is showcased?

Give the gift of a scrapbook. Scrapbook making has come a long way since our childhoods. Back then we clipped characters from cereal boxes and glued such finds onto cardboard. Now in arts and crafts chain stores, there are books of all sizes, colored labels, and art work paraphernalia geared to creating unique collectible books.

Get your child started creating scrapbooks. Suggest a theme

like leisure or travel, or favorite things or wish lists. If your child is on a sports team or part of a theater group, have him make a scrapbook on behalf of the team or club. This will prime him to document personal triumphs, efforts, and setbacks. You will be introduced to the personalities and passions that are part of his life. The possibilities are endless, as endless as the kind of information you'd like your child to share with you.

Encourage the art of collage. A collage is a mishmash of photograph snippets, images clipped from magazines or books, phrases. All are assembled in a shape. Collages have a theme. They can feature your daughter's friends (or nemesis) and the activities they do together such as birthday parties or sleepovers. Or a collage can depict a family by including relatives past and present in a family tree. A collage can record a child's past, present, and the future he envisions for himself. Or a collage can be focused on detailing all the aspects of a child's personality—hobbies, favorite stars or celebrities, fashion choices, and so forth. A collage can be assembled in an afternoon on a rainy day or it can be something that grows continually in any allotted space.

This pastime is especially useful for young adolescents. They take comfort in feeling a part of something—of a family or of a group. So constructing such a collage of family or friends or a team reinforces for them that sense of belonging. As you examine the collage in progress, ask questions about its components. Your child will volunteer inside information on what makes him laugh or feel empowered. You can also add information as you inject your memories of the people, places, and things pieced together in her design.

Always purchase the school yearbook. Most schools annually publish a yearbook. It is primarily put together by students and faculty advisors for the graduating class. Yet it also contains class photographs of every grade level in the school. There are group pictures of sports and club activities. And, oh, those candid shots of kids falling asleep in class or giggling in the hallways—these are favorites of children from nearly all the grades in the school. Kids absolutely love yearbooks. They love looking for their friends or their own picture. From year to year they like to see how people change.

If you get your child an annual yearbook, it's guaranteed you will be treated to a verbal blow-by-blow of the contents by your child. Before you know it, you will be learning which boy your daughter had a crush on at the beginning of school. Or which student your son envies. The class eccentric, flirt, brat, or bully—these and more will be pointed out. Chances are your child will get out last year's yearbook to show previous pictures of that cute boy or that bratty girl. Your children will have endless conversations with siblings about their friends. The secrets you will become privy to are worth whatever the price of the yearbook.

Provide a camera. Every child is a potential shutterbug. You don't have to buy your kids a pricey digital camera. Cameras come in all price ranges. Or you can simply opt for a cheap disposable. Letting children take photographs encourages them to capture the characters, events, and places they find worth re-membering. Having film of their lives is a record made by them that is readily available to you. Consider video cameras, too.

A picture, as they say, is worth a thousand words. A picture can also trigger another thousand words as your child narrates more.

Cameras, collages, scrapbooks, yearbooks, bulletin boards—these enable and motivate your child to express herself and re-veal all the details of her life *voluntarily*. Think humint again. These ideas put you on the receiving end of lots of secret in-formation without having to snoop for it. Such strategies bring your child into focus more clearly. Best of all they bring the two of you together rather than at odds the way snooping tends to do.

Too Much Information— The High Cost of Snooping

When it comes to your child's room, frankly you can never really know enough, acquire enough humint. Yet in the quest to treat your child's debris-laden space like a dig, how far can you go? Many of us have a hard time drawing the privacy line.

One parent asked, "Is it okay to read everything? I find notes my daughter has scribbled. I feel if she doesn't do a better job hiding this stuff then I have the right to read it. Am I wrong?"

Yes. Beware. Too much retrieved data can lead you into du-bious circumstances. We'll let the mother of a twelve-year-old boy show you the downside of ferreting out too much:

"I picked up my son's backpack. As I plopped it into his

bedroom some papers spilled out. To my surprise there were four pages of notes (front and back) that he and a girl had written back and forth. Along with the usual 'Does she like me?' stuff that you would expect to see, my son brags. He claims he spent a thousand dollars on concert tickets for girlfriends—three front row seats to Britney Spears. NOT! He went with his dad and a pal. Next he writes that he's been shot twice in the past by jealous ex-boyfriends of his gal pals. He claims to get a hefty allowance of fifty dollars a week to spend on any whim he desires. I'm guessing that he wants to look good to the other kids/girls. He's not very social with other kids his own age. I'm afraid he will be humiliated for his tall tales. I want to talk to him about this, but given how I got this information—how can I do that?"

The opportunities to eavesdrop by reading notes you find lying about or listening at the bedroom door to conversations are more than ample. Nearly all young adolescents are furious communicators. No sooner do they leave their peers at school when they seem to be in need of getting back in touch. Sneaking a look at or a listen to communiqués can unearth more than you bargain for. If you discover that your child is exaggerating, being cruel, lost in a crush or in a funk, you can't confront him without admitting you snooped.

Are you a snoop or a sneak? In our survey, 37 percent of ten- to fifteen-year-olds know you snoop. Parents confessed to going through the contents of the room, the closet, secret hiding places, and to following up with others on "the story" they hear from their child.

When you snoop, you drive your middler further away from

you at a time when you are needed the most. This is a time when our children are trying to figure out who they are and how to proceed in a new world. These early adolescent years are times of high insecurity, fragile self-esteem, and an obsession to fit in.

Meanwhile, conscience is forming. Your child is in the process of incorporating ethics into his very own personal portfolio. Young adolescents, and that means yours, watch parents like hawks. Their gaze analyzes your values and puts your character to the test. Then they decide which standards and rules merit imitation. Never forget that you are teaching by example every minute of every day.

Ideals are being mulled over as the middler brains grow and grasp abstract ideas. Amid all this growth, kids try out new psychic costumes and dubious ways of relating to one another. It is a trial-and-error process. We all learn more from errors. They are entitled to this private life even when it isn't admirable.

What we are saying is that you shouldn't seek to know everything. Give your young adolescent some slack here. You sought to know your baby and your toddler thoroughly. It was easy to check and recheck every detail—how she behaved in the sandbox or what outfit he put on in the morning. You knew she never ate string beans; he wouldn't wear turtlenecks. Your ten-year-old or fourteen-year-old isn't sure who he is these days. He is changing. He is growing up. You can't expect to know everything because your child isn't even sure of who he is or how to behave. He's a work in progress.

Take a wait-and-see approach. Mark Chamberlain, author

of *Kids Are from Jupiter: A Guide for Puzzled Parents* (Shadow
Mountain), remarks, "We have to be willing to allow our view
of our children to evolve. We have had certain experiences and
have created mental modes of our children based on those in-
teractions and observations. The problem is our children are
constantly changing, becoming new and different people, at
least in little ways, every day."

This is called giving them space. It's also called giving them
rope to hang themselves. It's also called giving them wings to
fly. They will need sturdy wings for their future. Think how
much more private your child's life will become. Get used to
accepting the fact that they, not you, control their destiny.

You are less likely to forge a harmonious relationship when
you don't honor the privacy zone of the bedroom. Take the high
road. The low road will go nowhere. In fact, it will cut you off
from your child and then open him up to going elsewhere for
intimacy and guidance. Probably to his peers. Remember: you
can push your child into a fortress of his own making or you
can orchestrate a sanctuary. With your behavior, you can build
walls or you can build bridges.

What You Should Do

Expect your child to develop a private life.
Set up reasonable guidelines and help organize stuff.
Enter armed with curiosity.
Empower your middler to update her digs.
Provide the means for your child to express himself
    willingly.

What You Should Not Do

Become suspicious when your child pulls away from you.
Nag about the messy room.
Ignore your child's bedroom.
Redecorate your middler's digs.
Gather information surreptitiously.

Chapter 2

The Body

"Nothing fits me right. I hate my body!"

My mom enters my room without knocking.
She doesn't wait until I say, "Come in,"
before bursting in. Sometimes I'm in the
middle of getting dressed and I don't want
anyone to see me. I would never do that to her.
Why does she think she can do that to me?

—Twelve-year-old girl

Remember those days when you powdered your child's bottom? You knew virtually every blemish and beauty mark on her body. You no longer have such uncontrolled access—and you shouldn't. Young adolescents, in the throes of puberty, are fiercely private about their developing bodies. While these feelings are normal and natural, behind this emerging modesty your child may be anxious and scared.

Young adolescents are works in progress. How your child looks at twelve or thirteen is not how she will remain. Yet popular culture sets an unrealistic standard. Middlers have little chance of pursuing Hollywood and Madison Avenue's vision of perfection—rail-thin models and beefcake musclemen. Many not only try but also threaten their health while doing so. Initially, a parent may be impressed by a child's desire to eat healthier or visit the gym more frequently. But when that desire turns into obsession, red flags go up. Even those children who don't resort to dangerous methods to change their looks may become depressed and withdrawn.

In this chapter we will talk about your young adolescent's body image. Whether you have a son or a daughter, do you know whom your child sees in the mirror? Whom is she comparing herself to? Is he upset that he doesn't measure up? How do you determine whether your child's preoccupation with looks is typical adolescent angst or abnormal behavior? What are the signs of an eating disorder? An exercise addiction? What strategies can you employ that will help your child without destroying your relationship?

Young adolescents are risk takers. They also live in the moment. Your daughter's immediate concern may be to look tan for that special dance on Saturday night. Visiting a tanning salon or baking in the sun for hours without sunscreen seems like a small risk to take. She isn't focusing on the life-threatening melanoma she could develop in the future. Similarly, your son's goal may be to get "buff," or "diesel." Taking steroids seems a reasonable shortcut, not a dangerous move.

Your challenge is to keep your child focused on long-term results while enduring short-term disappointments. Your information-gathering must endure limited access. Even a same-sex parent is often not welcomed into the dressing room. To find out what is happening with your own child, you will have to respect that privacy and find other ways to get the information you need to make sure your child is content and safe.

Developing Bodies—Growing Problems

The years from ten to fifteen are growth years—we might even say mega-growth years—for your child. During early adolescence, your son or daughter may grow twelve inches, a 20 percent jump for some.

There are gains to be made on the weight scale, too. Your ten-year-old daughter may weigh seventy-five pounds and, when she turns sixteen, 125 pounds. That weight hike injects a sour note into her sweet-sixteen celebration. If she is typical, she is poring over fashion magazines where six-foot-tall models weigh only 110 pounds (which, for that height, the government declares to be seriously underweight). How can she not help but panic? An oft-quoted survey of sixth-graders found that 60 percent of the girls and 40 percent of the boys worried constantly about how they look.

Some middlers mature faster than others. You probably notice this phenomenon when sizing up your child's friends and classmates. Some boys are tall and muscular, while others resemble the proverbial schoolyard victim. Similarly, there are girls who boast womanly figures, while others still long to wear their first bra.

Here are some things to expect during puberty:

Parts of the body grow at different rates. Hands and feet grow faster than arms and legs. You may wonder how your son could have outgrown those expensive new sneakers in just a few months. Also, the backbone grows more slowly than other bones. Some adolescents develop a lanky look. Other features—nose and ears, for example—may suddenly stick out, causing additional angst.

Hair grows in public and private places. Pubic and under-arm hair appear in some children as early as age nine. Hair begins to sprout in other areas—arms, legs, face—causing embarrassment and discomfort. Depending upon the coarseness and darkness of the growth, your child may be asking to shave.

Girls begin menstruation. Some girls get their periods as early as age nine or as late as age sixteen. While some girls are eager to reach this milestone, others have negative reactions ranging from anger to downright denial.

Moodiness makes some middlers miserable and miserable to be around. Hormones wreak havoc with middler moods. While parents understand that girls have mood swings related to menstruation, there is less understanding for boys who can't control their emotions. Yet your son's mood swings are real and may make him feel out of control.

Sweat glands develop. Small glands called eccrine glands are located throughout the body and help us control body temperature through sweating. "With the onset of sexual changes, and under the influence of sexual hormones, the apocrine glands also begin to proliferate," explains Dr. Ralph López, an adolescent pediatrician and author of *The Teen Health Book*. The apocrine glands are located in the "sexual" areas of the body—the armpit, because it has hair, and the groin. "When it comes to sweating these [apocrine] glands greatly outpace the eccrine glands," says López

Because young adolescents want immediate gratification, waiting for their bodies to catch up with their desires makes many of them unhappy. They know what they want to look like. They have the posters of their favorite sports heroes and stars tacked up on their walls. Why won't nature cooperate?

Here's where the trouble may begin. A middler may decide to jump-start the development process. Boys may hit the gym, lifting weights, working out. Girls attempt to lose weight, controlling food intake and exercising, sometimes excessively.

If only you could talk about body issues with your child. But here's the rub: middlers are loath to discuss the *p* word, namely, puberty. Like the white elephant in the middle of the room, your young adolescent's development is on everyone's mind, but no one wants to talk about it. You may be reluctant to discuss the sexual issues and your child is just downright embarrassed by the whole process. Just suggesting that your child needs to use deodorant may send him out of the room screaming. Yet talk about it you must.

In chapter five, you will receive guidance on how to talk

with your child about sex. Body image takes in some of that territory but encompasses other issues as well. Just knowing what to expect may help you put your child's reactions into perspective. That insight will calm you when you want to explode and reassure you when you become alarmed. Here are some common middler manias, along with suggestions for controlling your reaction and your child's:

"I don't need a bra." While some adolescent girls are thrilled to develop breasts, others go into denial. Girls who mature early are particularly self-conscious. Just changing for gym class produces trauma. One mother had this experience: "My daughter needed to wear a bra but got hysterical whenever I brought up the subject. One day I went to school to pick her up and a male teacher pulled me aside. She was wearing a T-shirt that, I admit, was a little revealing. He suggested that I take her shopping. I was *soooo* embarrassed! But his words spurred me to action. I told my daughter we were going to stop at the mall because I needed some things. Once there, I wandered into the lingerie department and selected several bras to try on myself. She began to look around at the colorful and sporty sets available and began to choose items for herself. We hit the dressing room together and left with our purchases and big smiles. She couldn't wait for the next morning so that she could wear her first bra."

"I don't want my period!" The average age of menarche has fallen to twelve from thirteen in 1960. A nine-year-old could still be playing with dolls when she gets her first period. Many girls are upset at reaching this milestone so early. Plan ahead. There are books aimed at young adolescent girls that discuss menstruation. If your daughter is shy about asking you questions, she may find the answers she needs by reading. Tell her that you are available to talk, even if "talking" involves more listening on your part. If she is upset, empathize with her. Share how you felt when you were her age.

Help her deal with the mechanics. Particularly if she is still in sixth grade, many elementary school bathrooms are not equipped with machines that dispense sanitary products. She may need to carry supplies or know that she can visit the nurse for help. Teach her how to track her period, keeping in mind that she may not be "regular" for some time. A visit to a doctor is a must, particularly if your daughter experiences discomfort when her period arrives.

Menstruation is a rite of passage, but stress to your daughter that this landmark does not mean she is ready for sexual activity. She may be receiving conflicting messages from her peers, so it's important that she hear your point of view.

"I'm never going to grow!" While some middlers mature too soon, others take forever—or so it seems to them. Girls worry about their figures, boys about their height. Watching their classmates shoot up or out is frustrating. Their smaller stature may make them ready targets for teasing and bullying. Remember the Tom Hanks movie *Big*? Ten-year-old Josh, eager to grow tall so that he could gain admittance to thrilling rides and impress the girls, had one wish: "I want to be big."

Even if your child could locate a Voltar wish-granting machine, his request would never be met as quickly. He will grow soon enough, however. Keep him focused on the long term, a challenge for in-the-moment middlers. Talk about your own experiences. Share family photographs. Schedule a doctor visit to assure your child he is normal and on schedule, albeit one that may lag behind his friends. And rent that Tom Hanks film. In the end, even Josh chose to take it slow.

"I don't need a shower." Middlers have a love-hate relationship with their bodies. They may love the idea of growing up. Dealing with it on a day-to-day basis, however, is not so easy. Cleanliness is a major issue. Your eight-year-old may have been able to get by with an evening bath and weekly shampoo. At ten, he may need to hit the shower every morning. The Johnson & Johnson baby powder now needs to be supplemented with a deodorant soap, antiperspirant, foot powder, and mouthwash.

If your child digs in his heels, be patient. Continue to stock his bathroom with the appropriate products and make gentle suggestions. Soon enough, when he discovers the opposite sex, this problem will evaporate.

Body Obsessions— The Female View

If your daughter could grow up in a vacuum, she would probably never experience a body image problem. If the only body she had to consider was her own, she would never suffer from comparison with others.

Unfortunately, that's not the real world. Outside influences are powerful in her life. While you may shelter her from the worst images, enough filters through to distort her vision. What are these sources and what are they telling her?

Women's fashion magazines. They shamelessly promote a female form that is difficult, if not impossible, for many to attain and keep. While the ideal woman's figure has fluctuated over the decades, the perfect silhouette keeps getting smaller and smaller. The average model, a size eight in 1985, by 2002 was a size two or zero. Ironically, the average woman's size is now fourteen.

Former models speak out about the agony of staying so thin. Many have confessed to eating disorders, substance abuse issues, and serious depression. Nothing, however, can reverse the trend to promote über-thin as the key to fame, fortune, and happiness.

Teen versions of adult fashion magazines. These find an eager and affluent market. While some of these publications run articles encouraging girls to love their bodies as they are, the models used negate that message. The fashions spotlighted— bare midriffs; tight-fitting, low-slung pants; and supershort skirts—are shown to advantage on waiflike teens.

Young adolescents, self-conscious, insecure, and looking for the fast route to popularity, make a gullible audience. While there are many reasons young adolescents develop eating disorders, you should not discount the tremendous impact these fashion images have on your daughter.

Pro-anorexia Web sites. Usually run by the sufferers themselves, they extol the virtues of losing weight and instruct how to drop the pounds. The advice is incorrect, irresponsible, and downright dangerous. Because of the laissez-faire nature that exists in cyberspace, critics have been unsuccessful in having these sites removed. Proponents cite First Amendment protection. In any case, some sites are ephemeral and would be hard to remove anyway.

How do young people find these sites? Some Web search engines locate these pages when key words like *eating disorder*, *anorexia*, or *bulimia* are typed in. (Some search engines have responded to critics and refuse to list these Web pages in their directories.) Word of mouth helps, too. One young person finds a site and e-mails the address to friends. With so many young adolescents on-line, these pro-anorexia sites can spread like wildfire.

Popularity of plastic surgery. Our aging population has become obsessed with staying young. That message has filtered down to our kids, who now seek out plastic surgery to improve their looks. According to *Seventeen* magazine, one-third of cosmetic procedures done in the United States are performed on patients eighteen or younger. In the magazine poll, 34 percent of the girls said they were considering breast implants or liposuction.

Pressure to assimilate weighs on immigrant girls. Eating disorders used to be the province of white upper- and middle-class girls. No more. Boys and ethnic minorities are falling prey.

Recent immigrants, hoping to fast-forward into American culture, are starving themselves thin. A March 12, 2000, article in the *Washington Post* noted that eating-disorder treatment centers in the Washington, D.C., Maryland, and Virginia area all reported an increased number of immigrant girls and young women coming in for treatment. Youth centers in Los Angeles and New York have set up groups so that Hispanic American adolescents can discuss their eating issues.

"There is a clear message in this country to young immigrant girls that, no matter how much you value your brain and your talents, being thin is more important than anything else," says Catherine Steiner-Adair, director of education, prevention, and outreach at Harvard University's Eating Disorder Center. She told the *Washington Post* that about one-fourth of her clients were American born but had parents from Latin America, Africa, the Middle East, or Asia.

Body Obsessions— The Male View

Women no longer have a monopoly on hating their bodies. More men are now secretly worried about how they look in a full-length mirror and are going to extremes—many painful, some dangerous—to achieve that perfect body.

How did this happen? A number of factors have come into play:

TV shows and movies. *Baywatch* and *Rambo*, among others, defined a new breed of hero, one whose physique put old-time film stars like John Wayne and Gary Cooper to shame. This new ideal body demanded large, sometimes huge biceps, a trim waist, and a rippled stomach, dubbed "six-pack" because the surface actually resembles a half-dozen cans.

World Wrestling Federation. The WWF, with high-profile stars like the Rock, reinforced the idea of the powerful, bulked-up male frame.

Athletes gain an edge with steroids. Former baseball major leaguer Ken Caminiti rocked the sports world after revealing in a 2002 *Sports Illustrated* interview that he was on steroids when he won the National League's Most Valuable Player Award in 1996. Caminiti defended his use of the illegal drug and alleged that steroid use was rampant in baseball.

Babe Ruth on steroids? Not likely. But the stakes in professional sports, and the financial rewards, are higher in modern times. With young players signing contracts worth hundreds of millions of dollars, the pressure to deliver at superhuman levels is overwhelming. For an athlete, the temptation to enhance performance by taking a drug becomes irresistible.

Young athletes, pushed to perform by parents and coaches, may view drugs as a convenient way to stay on top. There is routine drug testing on the professional and college level, but virtually none in middle or high schools. Not only do these drugs give some athletes an unfair edge, they also have serious health risks, especially for a growing young adolescent.

Magazines go after a male audience. Men now have their equivalents of the women's fashion magazines. And like their female counterparts, these magazines are filled with articles on how to achieve the perfect body and advertisements for products that guarantee a way to do so.

The gay movement encouraged bulking up. Many gay men, hoping to avoid the emaciated AIDS look, began to hit the gym in the 1980s. The advertising industry played up this new male sexuality on large billboards to sell everything from underwear to men's cologne. The strategy proved to be particularly effective. The male physique has been called the one crossover image that appeals to everyone—men and women—whether gay or straight.

Bodybuilding has become an institution. According to Arnold Schwarzenegger's book *The New Encyclopedia of Modern Bodybuilding*, the sport exploded in the 1980s. By 1990, the International Federation of Bodybuilders had more than 160 nations as members and had become the fourth-largest sports federation in the world. Competitive bodybuilding events began to attract larger numbers of both men and women. Schwarzenegger notes that in the first Mr. Olympia event held in 1965, the prize was merely a crown. By 1998, cash prizes had climbed into the six figures, thus providing incentive to many competitors.

Men perceive a threat to masculinity. With women now playing pro level sports previously reserved for men, moving up the corporate ladder, occupying positions of authority in government, and risking injury in daredevil stunts, many men are seeking a new definition of masculinity. If boasting superhuge biceps, pecs, and delts help to achieve that goal, the message is to lift on!

Getting to Know Your Way Around

You know what outside forces influence young adolescents. What are the possible disorders you may notice in your child?

Eating Disorders—Anorexia and Bulimia

The word *anorexia* comes from the Greek word *orexis*, meaning appetite. An-orexis, translates into the denying of appetite, particularly where food is concerned. Because young adolescents live in a food-saturated culture, self-starvation is not easy. If you've ever attempted a strict diet, you know how hard it is to restrict what you eat. For most anorexics, not eating involves more than the desire to be thin. Typically, the anorexic feels her life is out of control. How can she reassert her power? By controlling what she eats. You know what? That strategy works. What parent cannot notice when a child's weight drops precipitously? The risks are great—irreversible bone loss, organ damage, and death.

Bulimics also control their eating but in a different way. The bulimic eats, sometimes even binges, then makes a quick trip to the bathroom to purge. In addition to the health risks associated with anorexia, bulimics damage their teeth and esophagus, which are constantly bathed in stomach acids.

While 90 percent of eating disorder victims are girls, boys are making gains. Because anorexia and bulimia are not thought of as male diseases, some boys suffer in shame and silence. One dad in the Midwest says he first noticed his son's problem during a soccer game. "We noticed Kevin's lack of energy on the soccer field," his dad says. "Looking closer, there was something different about his body, his shape. He had begun to lose size and muscle mass."

Kevin's parents talked with him and discovered that he wanted a better body. Kevin, according to his parents, watches a lot of TV and was impressed by infomercials where male models with huge biceps and six-pack abs touted special diets and demonstrated workout equipment. "He was controlling his caloric intake, limiting himself to one thousand calories a day, eliminating all fats and almost all carbs," says his dad. In addition, Kevin was exercising obsessively—one hundred sit-ups and 150 push-ups a day." Even then, Kevin wasn't satisfied, trying to increase those numbers each time.

Kevin's dad knew that there was a genetic component at work, too. OCD—obsessive-compulsive disorder—runs in Kevin's family. Also, his school environment, homogeneous and very competitive, placed added pressure on Kevin to succeed. "Kevin is the number two athlete in the school," his father notes. "He wants to be number one. But the boy who edges him out has more natural ability." Dissatisfied with his ranking, Kevin pushed himself compulsively.

When confronted, Kevin was sad, then angry. He knew,

however, that he needed help. His parents insisted on a medical and psychological evaluation. A beginning exercise was showing Kevin pictures of various body types and asking him which he liked, which he did not like. "We were holding up the mirror to Kevin," his father says. "At that point, he had no muscle left, just skin and bones." Kevin began to see the harm he was inflicting upon himself. Reversing the situation, however, would take time and effort.

Because Kevin had lost so much weight, his doctor advised hospitalization. Once inside, he was required to consume 1,600 calories a day. If he did not reach that goal, he himself would have to learn how to insert a nasal gastric tube in order to supplement his diet. That factor jolted Kevin into action. "Not once did he need to do that," says his dad.

While in the hospital, Kevin talked to a psychologist. When he came home, his parents let him plan his own meals. "He wanted to eat healthier than we did," his father explains. "He kept a logbook of what he ate under the guidance of a counselor."

Months later, Kevin was back to eating with the family. While his dad is grateful for his progress, everyone understands that Kevin needs to stay on top of the situation. "He is still OCD," says his father. "Whatever Kevin does he will do to that level. *Moderation* is a word we use often."

Body Dysmorphic Disorder

Most young adolescents obsess about their looks occasionally, often before going to a special event. Usually the focus is something real—a pimple on the nose, too-large feet, frizzy hair. Comforting words may be enough to calm your child down and get her out the door.

Someone with body dysmorphic disorder, however, won't be dissuaded. This person worries about her appearance all the time. Ironically, the feature disparaged may look perfect to others. Yet this small, mostly invisible flaw, will consume her. She may look into the mirror and see that her hair is too thin or her nose too broad. No matter how many ways you tell her she looks fine, she won't believe you. The result? BDD can interfere, even ruin, her relationships, academic performance, and, ultimately, her life.

What are the warning signs of BDD? Here are some things to watch for:

- Staring into mirrors, windows, toasters, any shiny surface. Everyone glances into a mirror occasionally. Someone with BDD stares into every reflective surface possible.
- Going to extremes to cover the offending spot. This may include using excessive makeup or wearing scarves, sunglasses, large shirts, or whatever, to hide the problem.
- Constant comparison to others. These people may be in a magazine, on the street, or friends from school. But sizing herself up against the competition is relentless.
- Going to the doctors for treatments, even when the doctor advises against it.

- Seeking continual reassurance about the flaw. "Are you sure I look okay? No one will notice it?"
- Frequent anxiety. Those early-morning stomach-aches may indicate a problem.
- Avoiding social situations. If you know your child is self-conscious about a feature and she begins to shun invitations, you need to investigate.

Your child may need professional help to conquer BDD. One tactic strives to help the person resist the behavior associated with BDD, like frequent mirror checking or changing clothes, and encourages her to enter situations she previously avoided, like going to parties or having her photograph taken. This treatment also helps the person gain a more realistic appraisal of her appearance, possibly through looking at photos of others.

Acne and Skin Problems

Nothing can be more devastating—and common—during adolescence than an outbreak of acne. Acne is the most common skin problem in the country, affecting 85 percent of people at some point in their lives. At any given time, an estimated twenty million teens are battling breakouts.

In the past, parents regarded pimples as a rite of passage, unavoidable bumps on the road to adulthood. More recently, however, medical experts, armed with new topical treatments and drugs, maintain that these skin problems can be licked.

Here are some myths and truths about acne:

Certain foods cause you to break out. False. Acne is actually caused by blocked oil ducts that clog up the pores in the skin. These plugged pores can fill with bacteria and become inflamed. A whitehead is produced when there is enough oil and skin cells under the surface of the skin. A blackhead develops when the plug reaches the surface. The dark color is not from dirt but from melanin pigments, which give color to hair and skin.

Acne is hereditary. True. Skin problems do run in families. So, if you had serious skin problems as an adolescent, your child may, too.

Acne can be cured. False. Eruptions can be controlled but not eliminated forever. Even after adolescence, some people are plagued with acne.

Acne can scar the skin. True. Popping and picking pimples may leave scars later on.

Scrubbing the skin hard will minimize acne. False. It may feel good, but harsh rubbing may irritate the skin. Because the problem is more than skin deep, no amount of scrubbing will eliminate acne. Gentle cleansing with a mild soap will get rid of surface dirt and bacteria that could lead to future breakouts.

Stress causes acne. No one knows for sure, but some medical experts believe than an increase in adrenal steroids linked to stress may cause breakouts.

Young adolescents are very sensitive about acne. After all, how can your child face the world with pimples? Keep his feelings in mind when you approach him.

There are several good Web sites (www.caringforyourskin .com and www.pimpleportal.com) that offer both information and help. Suggest your Internet-savvy child pay a visit. He may come away with his own idea to seek out a dermatologist.

When you visit the doctor, allow your child to do the talking. The physician needs to know how your child feels about his acne. Because stress may sometimes be a factor, the doctor may want to inquire about his schedule, friends, and family demands. Of course, you should be consulted about treatment, but, again, let your child take the lead. If treatment will involve a daily regimen, your son needs to commit himself. He is more likely to do that if he makes the decision.

Trichotillomania—Pulling Hair

Young adolescents consider their hair their crowning achievement. Why then, would a child intentionally pull out her hair?

Trichotillomania (from two Greek words, *trix*, meaning *hair*, and *tillien*, meaning *pull out*) is a little-understood disease in which the sufferer plucks out her own hair, sometimes to the point of baldness. Because so many people hide this affliction, it's difficult to pinpoint how many have this disorder. Experts have estimated that anywhere between six to eight million people in the United States suffer from trichotillomania. Children, in fear of being detected, avoid amusement rides, sports, swimming, or dancing. A date would be unthinkable. What if a boy attempted to run his fingers through her hair?

As with BDD and eating disorders, medical experts suspect that trichotillomania is a form of obsessive-compulsive disorder. In effect, pulling hair allows the person to deal with stress, tension, and anxiety.

If you have watched your daughter twirl and tug on her hair absentmindedly, your suspicions may have been aroused. Some sufferers are able to restrict their hair pulling to one area of the head, which can be covered up with longer hair. A tip-off can be an abnormal amount of hair in the shower, bathtub, in wastebaskets, or on her hairbrush.

Treatment will involve therapy with medication. Behavior modification is used to break dependence upon this destructive habit.

Body Piercing and Tattoos

Piercing and tattoos used to be reserved for sailors and bikers. No more. So many people, young and old, famous and infamous, now boast body piercings and tattoos that the shock factor has gone way down.

That doesn't mean, however, that the risks associated with these procedures have disappeared. Anytime a needle pricks the skin there is the danger of serious infection, hepatitis C, or HIV. While that nose ring or tongue barbell can be easily removed, getting rid of a tattoo is more difficult. Even Johnny Depp chose to change Winona Forever to Wino Forever, rather than submit himself to the pain of having the tattoo totally removed.

Of course, middlers live in the moment. Your daughter can't envision a time when she won't want that rosebud on her breast or the ring through her navel. While some states have laws requiring permission before minors can be pierced or tattooed, inventive middlers can usually find a place that will skirt the law. One mother tells this story: "My daughter told me that four girls in her class got their navels pierced. I ran into one of the mothers and told her I was surprised she gave her permission. I was even more surprised to find out she hadn't and didn't even know!"

Take a preventive approach. "If you aren't going to be happy if your teen comes home with a tattoo, make this clear to your teen now," advises Dr. López. As for piercings, he says: "Tell kids that piercing hurts, that it leaves permanent holes, and that you do not consider it something that, as parents, you can allow."

Tanning

Sun-kissed skin is still in. Only one-third of 10,079 teens in a 2002 survey say they routinely use sunscreen and 10 percent used a tanning bed. Researchers at Boston University were stunned that teenagers consider a glowing tan worth obtaining at the risk of skin cancer.

More than one million Americans develop skin cancer each year. Medical experts have identified excess sun exposure as the leading cause of melanoma. Not only do young people seek out the sun unprotected, but also they visit tanning salons in between trips to the beach to keep up those bronze tones.

Popular female rock and film stars, whose persona includes conveying that sun-struck image, have been blamed for the youthful obsession with tans. (Previous generations may have worshiped the sun, too, but the link with cancer was tenuous back then.) Medical warnings about skin cancer have fallen on deaf ears. Two prestigious organizations, the Centers for Disease Control and the American Cancer Society, urge people of all ages to use sunscreen and avoid tanning beds. Sunburns in childhood have been shown to significantly increase the risk of developing skin cancer later in life. If she still wants that glow, look for makeup that can mimic a tan or self tanners.

A Body of Evidence— Clues and Cover-ups

You can't get into your child's head to truly know what he is thinking when he looks in the mirror. You go your opposite ways during the day. You can't follow him around to see what he eats and what he does. Even at home, your frame of reference is limited. How can you determine if your child has a problem? By watching when and where you can, without appearing to be too intrusive. Surprisingly, middlers scatter clues everywhere. While they often attempt to cover up, even a bumbling Inspector Clouseau would be able to gather the necessary facts. What follows are some situations you may have already experienced, along with some advice on what to do.

Your daughter is constantly announcing she is on a diet, but you never notice she is cutting back. She doesn't need to lose weight. Should you be concerned? Among your daughter's peer group, it's cool to be dieting. Unfortunately, this pack mentality pushes some girls, who shouldn't be restricting their intake, to cut back. The good news is that one study of 240 middle school girls found that many talk the talk without following through. Mimi Nichter found in her three-year study that half the girls never dieted for more than a few days. Those few who did lost less than ten pounds.

Don't overreact when your daughter announces her diet plans. Keep a watch. Chances are after a few days she will resume her normal eating patterns.

If your daughter seems determined to diet, work with her. Too many young adolescents start with a simple diet plan— eat less, exercise more—that can quickly spiral out of control. In fact, she may not need to eat less, just differently. Encourage her not to shun fats or carbohydrates. These are essential for her to have energy and satisfy hunger. Instead suggest she eat the foods she loves, just in reasonable amounts. She won't feel guilty when she has that occasional cookie or ice cream.

Your daughter announces she is a vegetarian. Young adolescents, concerned about the environment and animal rights, may opt for a vegetarian diet. Your child may be one who is driven by the desire to do the right thing. Make sure your child gets enough protein without eating meat.

Be watchful, however, that she doesn't use vegetarianism

as an excuse to stop eating. Make sure you offer her enough alternative food choices so that she finds something tasty to tempt her. You might want her to take a more active role and plan and cook some of her own meals or for the family to try. For menu ideas, try *Vegetarian Cooking for Everyone*, by Deborah Madison.

If she does stop eating, her meatless strategy may be covering up an eating problem. Talk with her about your concerns.

After each meal, your daughter heads for the bathroom. This behavior should raise a big red flag. Don't waste time. Schedule a doctor appointment immediately as a first step toward getting your daughter help.

You find over-the-counter laxatives, sleep-aids, and herbal supplements in your son's room. Your child may be using laxatives as a diet aid. Any weight lost, however, is apt to be water weight. And prolonged use of laxatives can disrupt his system and invite stomach and colon problems.

Herbal dietary supplements, flying off the shelves in health food and vitamin stores, are not regulated by the Food and Drug Administration. No one knows whether these products work or, more important, whether they are safe.

Young adolescents, eager for a quick fix, have provided these herbal marketers with a new clientele. Particularly suspect are supplements that contain ephedra, a Chinese herb also known as Ma Huang. Popular weight-loss products that list ephedra as an ingredient have been blamed for serious health problems, even deaths.

Because ephedra is a stimulant, insomnia can result. Sleep aids in a young adolescent's room may be a tip-off.

Talk with your child about these products. Read the labels with him, pointing out the ingredients that may be harmful. If he doesn't trust your opinion, make an appointment with your pediatrician, who can explain the dangers more specifically.

Your child's mood swings—from happy to sad, from content to angry—leave you reeling During puberty hormones rage, so a certain amount of moodiness is to be expected. A child whose mood swings are constant and intense, however, may be in trouble. He may be abusing alcohol or drugs. Or, as Kevin's father discovered, he may be in the throes of an eating disorder. "He had mood swing changes that we couldn't ignore," he says. Keep in mind that a serious problem could be surfacing. It isn't uncommon for bipolar disorder also known as manic-depressive illness, to emerge during these years.

After visiting a friend's house, your daughter returns home, her clothes reeking of smoke. According to the Centers for Disease Control, 40 percent of white and Native American girls, 33 percent of Hispanic girls, and 12 percent of African American girls confess to smoking cigarettes. While many girls smoke to fit in among their peers, some have a more specific reason for lighting up: they hope that inhaling smoke will prevent them from inhaling food.

If you detect smoke on your daughter's clothes, you will want to deal with the smoking issue first. Don't stop there. Investigate whether she hopes smoking will help her diet. Help her understand that, healthwise, she is playing with fire. She may lose weight but become addicted to tobacco and wind up down the road with serious health problems.

You find empty boxes of cookies, Twinkies, candy, potato chips, and popcorn when you clean your son's room. Unless your son threw a party in his room the night before, he may be a secret binge eater. Young adolescents who binge often experience tremendous shame and so hide the evidence from family and friends. Mention to your son your surprise and listen to his explanation. If you aren't satisfied, you will need to keep a closer watch.

Your daughter has a cute figure but is always hiding it under large, oversize clothing. It's possible your daughter is being sexually harassed at school. Some girls, to hide their developing bodies from probing eyes, wear oversize clothing to minimize scrutiny from boys. If she already is self-conscious about her figure, such teasing will only make matters worse. Does she seem withdrawn, depressed? If so, she may indeed be a target. Talk with her to find out why she is dressing this way. If she remains mum, you may need to talk with other parents or her teachers to see what is happening in school.

You daughter takes forever to get dressed for school or a social event. She tries on dozens of outfits, changes her hairstyle several times, even obsesses over which earrings to wear. Most adolescents suffer indecision when getting dressed, particularly when they know members of the opposite sex will be present. But if your child's behavior is ongoing and beginning to interfere with her schedule, she may be trying to deal with body dysmorphic disorder. Sometimes BDD sufferers agonize over what they will wear, hoping to cover up perceived flaws. Check over the list of BDD symptoms to see if there are other warning signs.

You know that your son is overweight, but you hesitate to suggest a diet. While some middlers starve themselves, others can't stop eating. Americans are getting heavier, and, unfortunately, children are among the worst performers. Obesity and diabetes, historically medical conditions associated with older people, now plague our youth. The reasons are many but can be summed up essentially by pointing out that our kids eat more (and less healthfully), and exercise less.

You can help at home this way:

- Don't buy junk food. Satisfy your family's craving with air-popped popcorn.
- Drink water, not soda. Each can of cola adds 150 calories to your child's diet and no nutritional value. If she balks at plain water, flavor it with a small amount of fruit juice.
- Avoid artificially sweetened products. Research has shown that these items merely fuel the urge for more sweets.
- Stock your refrigerator with bite-size fruits and vegetables. Baby carrots, berries, cherries, and grapes are loaded with vitamins and fiber.

- Choose protein. When your child is prowling in the kitchen, suggest cheese, eggs, peanut butter, or nuts, which will satisfy his hunger longer.
- Avoid convenience foods. Whether fast-food or something that can be zapped in the microwave, most prepared items are high in fat, salt, sugar, and calories.
- Don't be fooled by low-fat products. Often these are high in calories.
- Set a good example. If you eat healthy foods, you will have less trouble getting your kids to follow.
- Monitor the TV. Often those hunger pains follow a TV advertisement for junk food. Turn off the set and play a board game instead.

Taboos—
A Body of Secrets

You may be well-intentioned where your child's body privacy is concerned. Nevertheless, you may find it's sometimes easy to cross that privacy line without even thinking. Here are some situations to avoid:

Bursting into her room or the bathroom while she is getting dressed or naked. You may be wondering whether your child has developed pubic hair yet. Chances are she won't let you see. You may get a glimpse if you walk in on her unannounced (and really, what's the big deal? She was never this shy about being naked in front of you).

One doctor tells this story: "A mother brought her fourteen-year-old daughter in to see me. The mother—stylish, thin, and petite—ushered her large-framed young adolescent in, telling me, 'Her vulva doesn't look right.' Then she added, 'Her breasts have ugly stretch marks.' How many years of therapy lie ahead as the girl in question shies away from having sex because of her ugly body. I took the mother aside, knowing full well that I'd never see her in my office again, and chided her for inspecting her daughter's vulva and breasts. I told her that such behavior is totally inappropriate."

Staying in the doctor's office while she is being examined. Speaking of the doctor's office, it's time you took a seat in the waiting room. If the doctor needs to talk with you, he'll call you in afterward.

Once your child hits puberty, you may want to consider switching to an adolescent pediatrician. "When my son turned thirteen, he felt embarrassed sitting in a waiting room with babies and toddlers," says one mother. "Also, his pediatrician wasn't good about closing the door when he was undressed and he didn't like the way she addressed everything to me, not to him. We made the switch to a doctor who specializes in adolescents, and he has developed a good relationship with him. I no longer know everything he tells the doctor, and I don't want to."

If you need help finding an adolescent specialist in your area, you can contact the Society of Adolescent Medicine, 1916 NW Copper Oaks Circle, Blue Springs, MO 64015, phone, 816-224-8010, Web site, www.adolescenthealth.org.

Accompanying her into the department store dressing room.
She may be self-conscious about trying on clothes with you in
the room. Wait until you are invited.

Placing food on her plate in an effort to get her to eat. This
tactic is sure to backfire. Remember, eating disorders are about
control. If you try to control what your child eats, she will dig
in her heels to win the battle.

In the same vein, try not to scrutinize everything she eats.
Don't count her calories, monitor how many helpings she is
taking or how large they are, or make comments about her eating style. She may quickly lapse into an eating disorder to avoid
your intrusion.

Insisting she get her hair cut a certain way. A mother who
visited us on-line said she argued with her daughter every time
she needed a haircut. "My daughter's face shape is just like
mine and we look best in a pageboy cut with bangs. But she always complains when it's time for a haircut. I'm tired of the
battles."

Stop splitting hairs. How your daughter wears her hair
should be her decision. Forcing her to wear a certain style will
make her miserable and rebellious. She may look for control in
other areas of her life and develop a worse problem that will
make the hair battle seem minor—which it is.

Dictating what she can wear. The youth culture has its own
style. That fashion may not be to your liking (chances are your
parents didn't like your clothes, either). Give your child some

leeway here. Find something about his fashion choices to praise. "Gee, that's an interesting combination. Who would have thought that zebra stripes would go with plaid?"

Undergarments that we kept hidden, young people now flaunt. Boxer shorts peer out from your son's low-slung jeans and bra straps grace your daughter's shoulders. If you push too hard, your child will just change at a friend's house. Go shopping with your child and help her to make choices that respect her style and your guidelines. Particularly with a daughter choosing provocative clothing, ask, "What message are you sending with this outfit? Will you be able to handle the consequences?"

Making comments about her appearance. How many adolescents were launched on an eating disorder or body obsession after hearing one simple criticism? If you have a bona fide objection—for example, you feel your daughter's pants are too tight—phrase it the proper way. "Those pants must have shrunk the last time we washed them. Perhaps you can try another pair and I can take those back to the store."

Hiding your child's body image problem from others. If your child is struggling with a body issue, you may not want this news broadcast to everyone. Going to extreme lengths to cover up, however, may make your child paranoid and send the wrong message, namely that you feel your child has done something wrong and shameful. He will never recover with that burden to shoulder.

Take your cues from him. He may want to confide in a few

close friends and also want you to talk with their parents. That's what Kevin's dad did. "We shared with Kevin's friends, boys and girls," his dad says. "We also shared with friends we trusted."

Hoping to reach out to other families, Kevin's dad also put out the word at his company. "We have five thousand employees, and I think there must be other parents out there going through the same thing," he says. "We can help."

Not establishing sibling boundaries. Your twelve-year-old may have to share a room with a younger sibling and have to retreat to the bathroom to avoid the prying eyes. A younger child is going to be naturally curious about the changes her sister is going through. After all, she's next! But talk with both of them about setting up some boundaries. Perhaps each one deserves some alone time during the day when she can change without being interrupted. The younger child will appreciate this approach when she hits puberty.

Too Much Information——When to Hold Back

There are areas that should remain private for your child as far as body image is concerned. Even if you suspect the worst—an eating disorder, substance abuse problem, or another issue— you need to respect your child's boundaries.

Kevin's father struggled. "We respected his privacy, but losing the weight was such a public, visual thing, at the time we all invaded his privacy," he says. While Kevin kept a food log, his parents never read it. "We did give him privacy with regard to that," says his father. Kevin's parents would accompany him to his counseling sessions, but they would sit outside. "With the counselor, 80 percent of the sessions were just the two of them," Kevin's father says. "My wife and I would come in at the end, just so the counselor could bring us up-to-date, but not to invade Kevin's privacy."

This dad summed up his attitude in a philosophical way: "There are things you need to know. If you live in a world of things it's nice to know, you have it a lot tougher." Kevin's parents needed to know he had an eating problem; they didn't need to know every one of his innermost thoughts as he wrestled with his demons.

Respecting those boundaries, Kevin's dad says, helped bring the entire family closer together. "We really respect each other," he says. "We're sharing more than we would have if we had not gone through this experience."

What You Should Do

Respect your child's desire for privacy surrounding body issues.

Encourage your child to eat healthy food and to exercise.

Keep alert to signs that may signal an eating disorder.

Teach your child media literacy, to watch fashion with a skeptical eye.

What You Should Not Do

Sneak peeks to gauge your child's development.
Try to control what your child eats.
Make comments about your child's appearance.
Come between your child and the doctor.

Chapter 3

Friends

"They're my friends, don't criticize them!"

There are some things about my friends
that I don't tell my parents.

—Twelve-year-old girl

As boys and girls enter early adolescence, Mom and Dad seem to get ejected from *the-most-important-person-in-life* post. A best friend or two is anointed instead. Loyalties shift. A young adolescent chooses friends, not family, with whom to spend time and share confidences. (The child covets and constructs an exclusive, very private life.) Mom, Dad, and even siblings are deliberately rejected.

Being outside your child's secret society is tough. Involuntarily, you flash back to that same freckle-faced girl turning five.

She volunteered *everything* about her friends—who made her crack up or who made her cry. It's painful, not to mention worrisome, when your young adolescent clams up. Building a separate, private life—and protecting it—is part of growing up and away from parents.

It's easy to know too little about a child's friends. Ditto for what goes on inside those inner social circles. Not getting the scoop legitimately, parents entertain espionage-like tactics. "My parents snoop on me, yes," claimed a twelve-year-old girl from New England. "When they're the only ones home, I hear them hanging up the phone ever so gently, or worse, breathing when my friends are talking to me."

Are such breaches excusable? How much are you entitled to know about your child's friendships? In this chapter we will tackle the friends frontier. We map out an effective way to scope out the character of friends without criticizing, a negative nagging that only triggers middlers to get defensive. We will discuss supervision and trust, issues that go to the heart of parenting older children. You can grant your child the privacy in her social life that she is entitled to, and still create a privacy trust between the two of you.

Friends Are Partners in Survival, Not Partners in Crime

What do ten- to fifteen-year-olds whisper to one another out of your earshot? It boils down to sharing pieces of the self. As their brains grow, perspective outgrows what happens inside the family. Middlers seek out a larger world filled with exciting people and possibilities. They enlist peers in this coming-of-age drama because *only* peers share this passage. Peers become comrades in a survival challenge. To one another they reveal personal thoughts and experiences, secret fears or hidden pains. Children at this stage embark on a compare-and-contrast game with acquaintances in order to figure out how they stack up, where they fit, and who they are. Self-discovery is at the core of these new liaisons.

The agenda for preadolescents resembles gossip. What happened at school, who smiled at whom, or what she got on that math quiz—such is the usual minutiae exchanged. And yet, young adolescents do flirt with risky behaviors such as alcohol, drugs, and sexual experimentation. Their communications explore and detail the choices surrounding such adventures.

When a parent feels shut out, those new friends can look like *the enemy*. Rather than viewing these peers as partners in the growing process, you might wind up viewing them negatively as partners in potential crimes. Your imagination can spin horrendous scenarios. You can feel as if these young strangers have launched a hostile takeover on your home front. Don't let paranoia set in.

As a child moves from ten on through later adolescence, parents have to juggle stepping back, letting go, and monitoring. Mothers and fathers need to cultivate an open mind and have confidence in a child. Having friends is important. The child who has none has a lonely life. Realize though, that children behave differently in the company of other young adolescents. Experts and research findings underline this fact: young adolescents get into more dilemmas in packs. They do things *together* that they would *never* do alone.

Consider this e-mail from a parent who asked us for advice:

"A few nights ago, my fifteen-year-old son and a couple of his friends went out to shoot a video. They put together a great video for a school project that my son proudly showed me. I didn't blink an eye until I happened to look at the whole tape left in the camera. I was appalled by the language, but the content was far worse. My son along with his pals filmed practical (dangerous) jokes on automobile drivers including shooting out a streetlight with a pellet gun. My son found me in tears looking at the film and he broke down. He is a great kid but when he gets together with these boys there can be trouble! What do I do?"

What an immature adolescent brain conceives of as a funny prank can escalate into a major disaster. The broken streetlight could translate into a two-car collision, fatalities, and manslaughter charges.

Getting to Know Your Way Around— The Pack and the Pack's Code

Your job is to get to know your child's friends. You cannot pick and choose her companions, but you can and should offer guidance. Getting inside the heart, the habits, and the hangouts of your child and the friends she makes will enable you to assess her social adjustment, her safety, and the likelihood of being implicated in risky behaviors.

Young and older adolescents themselves are notorious for not being able to assess risks within situations or with regard to peers. Before you can build an argument against a friend and advise your child, you need to get a handle on her friends. Do certain friends come with liabilities and secrets, putting your child under pressure to lie? For some parents, answering that question is easy because they've known these same boys and girls forever. However, many children change friends during middle school. This is a time when boys and girls abandon childhood pals. Before the emotional dust settles, the child is off and running with a new best friend or a new crowd. Who are these people?

The biggest obstacle to your getting an inside take on this secret society is probably your own child. Middlers are protective of friends and fiercely defensive when you criticize these friends. Parents often judge by what is on the outside—a boy's demeanor, an easy smile, or a rebellious smirk; a girl's style, fashionable or suggestive. While expression and looks are telling, going deeper is in order for a more comprehensive conclusion.

Your child may be open about her group of friends. The social scene may unfold right in your own living room. You can see for yourself how healthy her friendships are and whether or not her acquaintances are good and kind people.

However, many children this age don't open up about what role they play in the social scene. Cliquish behavior is commonplace during middle school. What if you suspect that your child is being victimized by a bully, or worse, is bullying others? Suppose she is following the lead of mean personalities? You may find out or suspect that this group is using drugs or drinking. Is there any way you can predict trouble ahead *even before* cruel behavior or substance or alcohol abuse kicks in? There is a way to identify the quality of relationships and the risks within your child's social circle.

We want to show you how to compile a profile of your child's friends, one that goes beyond first impressions and stereotypes. The following framework can guide you. It's based on a study of delinquents that has proven to hold insightful lessons for all parents.

In 1999, James Garbarino, Ph.D., published *Lost Boys: Why Our Sons Turn Violent and How We Can Save Them*. Dr. Garbarino summed up typical delinquents: "They lose their way in the pervasive experience of vicarious violence, crude sexuality, shallow materialism, mean-spirited competitiveness, and spiritual emptiness." While such influences surround all of our children some of the time, apparently they poison these especially vulnerable kids.

Dr. Garbarino identified three anchors that rescued lost boys. The first is spirituality or having a spiritual agenda or focus. The next is affirmation, getting emotionally stroked by a parent. The third is hope, having a dream and the confidence to think that realizing a dream is possible. These anchors counteracted polluting influences.

We suggest you take these anchors to heart. Pay attention to how these anchors play out, or don't, in the life of your own child and in the lives of your child's acquaintances and best friends. Use them as a measuring stick.

Can you see these threads in your own family life with all of your children? Observe your child's companions. Tactfully ask questions about their religious membership or ethical commitments, their parents, their home life, and their ambitions and goals. For instance, "Does Britney volunteer like you do for Habitat for Humanity?" Or "Does Danny's father work on his baseball swing with him at home?" Or "Jenny's outfits are so wild, does she have her sights set on fashion or the music business?"

This triad of spirituality, affirmation, and hope can serve as a resourceful blueprint. It can give you a concrete sense of what you are doing right, and what your child is doing right. And it can highlight vulnerability. When these values, goals, and experiences are missing among your child's friends, watch closely because

A Young Adolescent Without a Conscience or Ethical Touchstone Has No Checks or Balances

Children who attend religious services at a church, synagogue, or mosque have a fundamental spiritual life. They bring a compass of right and wrong to the group. Organized religion is only one face of ethics. There are others, such as community service. Many young people volunteer or participate in fundraising efforts in and out of school. There are environmental groups, events like runs or walks to fight cancer or diseases.

Does your child and/or his group spend any time soul-searching or doing service? Does their emotional portfolio include compassion and caring along with the usual adolescent emotions of feeling invincible and looking for adventure? Does your child or do his friends set an example for younger siblings or imitate the positive modeling set by an older brother or sister?

A Young Adolescent Who Gets No Love from an Adult Seeks Attention by Acting Out Negatively

For children to thrive they need an adult who loves them, one who genuinely cares about the quality of their emotional life. A child who has this feels accepted and lovable, a foundation upon which self-confidence grows. Adult attention bestows stability and security. The adult can be a parent, but could be a teacher, community leader, or an older sibling.

Judge whether or not your child's friends are loners. Are they alienated from parents? Does a coach, teacher, uncle or other adult fill in the gap? In today's world of two-parent wage earners, single parents, and stepfamilies, too many children aren't close to any adult. No adults are there to cheer a teen on at a sporting event or when he receives a commendation at an assembly. Do your daughter's friends go to the mall with their mom? Do they mention watching DVDs or attending a concert with a parent? Do your son's friends go fishing or go anywhere with Dad? Or are they under the wing of a favorite coach or mentor?

Does the group choose to exclude and avoid adults? Some packs are rogue and never want adults around. Others welcome the presence of adults, and their rides to hockey games or out for hamburgers.

A Hopeless Young Adolescent Is a Reckless and Self-Destructive One

Every child needs to have faith in himself and his future. For a ten-year-old, this can mean he thinks he can make the wrestling team. For an older child, it translates into visions of herself becoming a dancer or a doctor. Adolescent hopes can be assorted, strange even. They can center on growing long hair or getting biceps, beating the villain in a video game, or winning a class election. The important component is that your child and the chosen friends have goals, accompanied by the belief that effort can make them happen. A child without hope is a potential bully, substance abuser, academic slouch, and/or vulnerable to depression or anger.

If there are friends of your child who worry you, create a mental watch list. If your gut screams negatives, find out more about the companion. Include him or her in activities that you do as a family. Ask teachers at school if this friend could be a bad influence on your child. Find out from your son or daughter what he or she likes about this person.

Forbidding a friendship doesn't work with an older child the way it can with a grade school one. It tends to incite rebellion. Opt instead for keeping a close watch on any friendship that concerns you.

Meanwhile, assess how the group behaves. Watch for the negative aspects of cliques: teasing, belittling, or back stabbing. If you see bullying, even if it's your child doing it or sanctioning it, raise the issue with her. (For more information on how to handle the social dynamics of cliques, take a look at our book *Cliques: 8 Steps to Help Your Child Survive the Social Jungle*.) Discover what the group loves and hates collectively. What is its definition of a good time? Some packs center around parties and playing sports. Popularity may be their defining value. Other circles revolve around hobbies—skateboarding, chess, even academics. How would you rate their interest in material stuff? Is the group totally into clothes, worldwide wrestling matches, electronics, endless new video games, collections of something? When they mouth lyrics in unison, what sentiments lie behind the music? Knowing the values of your child's youth culture is indispensable. What surrounds your child's group says reams about her friends and the developing mores and values of your own child.

You have to look not only at the face of your child and her friends but further into their hearts and their souls. You cannot calculate whether these friends are unworthy until you know who they are.

Diagram Leisure Time

Furthermore, you need to get a handle on what happens when you are not looking.

Your twelve-year-old says, "See ya, Mom. I'm going out."

You ask, "Where?"

He answers, "Nowhere."

You follow up, "With whom?"

He responds, "Nobody."

You quip, "How long will you be?"

He says, "I don't know, not long."

You want to know more. "What will you be doing?"

"Just hanging out, what's the big deal!"

The above conversation is typical, but it doesn't reveal much at all. Being evasive is standard adolescent behavior. It doesn't mean your child is up to no good. Still, get a leg up on the comings and goings of your child whenever she goes off. You have a responsibility to monitor the who, what, when, and where of your daughter's life and the company she's in. This holds true whether you like your child's friends or whether you don't trust them entirely. It holds even when your child has little in the way of a social life because that, too, is a red flag possibly signaling clique or bullying problems. If this sounds as if we are stating the obvious, bear with us. Many parents are missing this point.

Ironically even as the dangers in our society escalate, parents are responding with less, not more, vigilance. Harvard University psychologist Dan Kindlon, author of *Too Much of a Good Thing: Raising Children of Character in an Indulgent Age*, (Talk Miramax Books) documented that half of the parents he surveyed characterized themselves as less strict than their own parents. Sixty percent characterized their children as very or somewhat spoiled. In between the lines of this research is an interesting implication. Parents are casting themselves as permissive or powerless, incapable or unwilling to set standards.

Hanging out *nowhere with no one for not long* is unacceptable. A major survey of ten thousand twelve- to seventeen-year-olds called "The National Longitudinal Study of Adolescent Health" tabulated risky habits including cigarette smoking, drinking, drug abuse, carrying guns and knives, and sexual activity. Dr. Robert Blum of the University of Minnesota, who served an instrumental role in analyzing the data, warned: "What young people do with their free time and how they do at school are the most important determinants for every risky behavior we studied—regardless of whether they were rich or poor, white or black or Hispanic, or come from one- or two-parent families."

Get specifics on your middler's destinations by asking and getting answers to: Where are you going? Who's going to be there? What will be going on?

Most young adolescents have routine hangouts. They can range from a best friend's home, to the local mall, a popular street corner, or the town beach or lakeside. Knowing our child's companions and their agendas is part of our job as parents. Try the following *do* and *don't* ideas to get in the know positively:

Do Introduce a Family Calendar of Events

Get a large calendar with lots of room for notes. Scribble in your own appointments monthly: Monday night PTA meeting. Friday afternoon lunch with Anne. Golf on Saturday. Sale at Old Navy. Map out community activities you want to attend from garden shows to plays and lectures. Jot in movies that you want to catch on cable. Have all of your children do likewise. If your daughter needs a ride to a sports event, ask her to mark the calendar so you will remember. Have them pencil in pizza parties, shopping plans, informal basketball games at the playground, everything. The practice ritualizes telling one another your plans in detail. This tally becomes the family's way of keeping in touch with one another's schedules. And it helps you keep tabs on your children.

Don't Use Siblings as Spies

This is a negative approach guaranteed to further isolate your young adolescent from brothers or sisters. Siblings are a natural resource and even a safety net for one another. That may be hard to believe because sibling rivalry heats up during early adolescence. Brothers and sisters do seem to bicker more. Even so, a curious, inexperienced, troubled, or confused child often feels more comfortable asking a sibling a question. If you distort the sibling bonds, you take away that resource.

Do Use Older Siblings as Chauffeurs

Most of us are busier than we want to be. If you can't attend a school event or do the car pool run, enlist an older sibling. This sets up a family framework that keeps you in the loop of your child's destination. (The only caveat here is if the sibling is a new driver. Make sure other parents know the driver is safe and capable.)

Host, Host, Host

Cultivating rapport and relationships with your child's friends is key. There are certain homes that become magnets for kids. Even if yours is not that home, invite your child's friends over. Create a pizza night. Welcome sleepovers. Watch movies. Get to know her friends.

Go to as Many Functions as You Can at School and in Your Community

Watching your child play a sport, play an instrument, participate in a community service event—any and all these offer you a glimpse into his social world. And a closer look at the company he keeps.

Cover-ups— When Even Good Kids Do Bad Things

Even when friendships are entirely harmless and normal, kids may opt for a few of these standard cover-ups.

Your Child Is Caught Sneaking Out

A few years ago, fourteen-year-old Jennifer Grimes of New Cassel, New York, aced this prank, stealing away at midnight to meet her friends on a nearby suburban street corner. Tragically, her *put-one-over-on-parents* lark proved fatal. Jennifer died in a freak accident, a drive-by shooting. When the police rang up her family, they insisted she lay sleeping upstairs.

Was Jennifer's sneakiness extraordinary? Not really. If you analyze TV shows and commercials, movies or music videos, teenagers sneaking out of the house is a familiar scenario. In *Dawson's Creek*, a popular teen drama, high school–age Dawson uses his second-story bedroom window as his parents use their front door. His friends climb in and out all the time. There's even a ladder leaning against the facade of the house to make it easier.

Your home isn't a TV show. Why would a fourteen-year-old fluff up a pillow and slither past the living room? Young adolescents are by nature thrill seekers. They love putting one over on adults just as they savor chastising you when a curse word slips from your lips or you do something hypocritical. A midnight rendezvous comes under the heading of extra time with friends at an age when they *never* have enough time with peers.

Still, every child who deliberately takes this clandestine route deserves to be dealt consequences so it won't happen again. A child on the streets late at night is in danger.

You Catch Your Child Lying

At one time or another during early adolescence, most girls and boys are caught in a lie. This is unnerving. Here is your child betraying you, your trust, your values. "What's next?" you ask yourself. "Is this the first lie or has she lied before?"

Accepting the reality that your child will try to pull the wool over your eyes is disappointing. Before you shake your head in despair, let's face some preliminary facts. If the truth be told, our children are mimicking us. Bella DePaulo, a psychology professor at the University of Virginia, specializes in research on lying. Asking adults to keep an honesty diary, she tallied that most of them lied once or twice a day—almost as often as they snacked from the refrigerator. Men and women lied in equal measure, in one-fifth of their social exchanges. The sexes differed on their motivations for not making honesty the best policy. Women lied to protect someone else's feelings.

Men typically stretched the truth to put themselves in a more favorable light.

Even if lying has seeped into our collective core, we cannot excuse dishonesty. In our survey, and during focus groups on privacy, we asked ten- to fifteen-year-olds, "Do you tell your parents the truth?" "Sometimes" announced a majority. Did anyone say "always"? A meager few. Don't despair, because no one said "never."

Our investigation mirrors the findings of other truth versus lying scales. In a 1998 poll of twenty thousand middle and high school students conducted by the Josephson Institute for Ethics, 88 percent of sixth- and seventh-graders admitted to lying to their parents. Older teens lied more, with 92 percent fessing up to the practice.

According to DePaulo, most children this age lie to protect their friends. Lying is particularly troubling behavior for young adolescents because it puts them at risk. Possibilities abound. A friend sneaks on to a pornographic site on the Internet. A best bud takes his first drink at a party. A girl pal takes her boyfriend's hand and leads him into the bedroom when her parents are at work to dabble in lust. Your child will never tell.

Lies take both active and passive forms. Some young adolescents will deliberately lie, as in "No, none of my friends would ever drink or do drugs." Others evade the truth. "I didn't say those mean things to Taylor." What's missing here? She knows who did. Or they leave out certain highly charged details. "We didn't do much at Nick's house, just played some video games and fooled around on the computer." No mention of any porn sites.

The secrecy code prevails among youth. As one almost-twelve-year-old girl told us "Some stuff going on parents just don't need to know." He or she will keep mum primarily because you are The Authority. Your role puts you in charge of the keys to the kingdom of punishment. More than one middler penciled in a variation on this girl's "I withheld information because I did not want to get into trouble."

Don't go overboard and assume your child is bound to lie. If you do sense your child is being less than honest, or if you do catch your child in a boldface lie, don't look the other way. Statistics suggest that women are superior to men at picking up lies. Does that mean mothers are better than fathers at sniffing out a sneaky preteen? Perhaps.

Make time to discuss this subject further. Choose a moment when you are not feeling furious or disappointed. You need to remain calm so you can learn whom the lie is designed to protect—your child or a friend.

Set the stage verbally. A useful strategy comes from a teacher we surveyed who suggests, "Explain to your child that it is important to be truthful. Tell her, 'As these years pass, and situations are of more import, we need to have a relationship where we can trust each other.'"

Remind your child that trust goes both ways. These are the years to bring honesty and trust into frequent conversations. Hold yourself to the same standard to which you hold your family.

Talk to older children about "protecting" younger ones. It is natural for your children to share private information with one another. Discuss appropriate bounds of privacy with older siblings. Tipping off a parent is not tattling. Explain how keeping a secret about misbehavior is not helping an adventuresome or troubled sibling.

Your Child Is Attending Frequent Sleepovers

"Mom, can Emily sleep over tonight?" Overnights is how middlers socialize. It is a fun and normal sign of development. Pajama parties celebrate birthdays for both genders. Your biggest concern may be not to let the group overdose on sweets and soda, a recipe for no sleep and a cranky hangover the next day.

Yet, a pattern may signal cause for alarm. As one parent reported, "I attended a talk required by my school for the parents of all athletes. My daughter was in ninth grade, almost fifteen. A guidance counselor point-blank told us to be suspicious of sleepovers. If a child *regularly* asks to sleep at another's home, it may be to disguise drinking or drug use."

Because an unsuspecting parent is not meeting the child at the end of an evening, Mom or Dad can't smell the beer on her breath, or observe signs of slurred speech or staggering. The best insurance is to call the other parents if you suspect that sleeping over is a cover-up.

Taboo Invasions——Distrust or Trust

If you aren't privy to your child's secrets, you probably bristle over the fact that other kids share much more with their parents. The next parent made that clear:

"I have a thirteen-year-old daughter who, I am finding out, DOESN'T tell me things that are going on in school. I think most of it is stuff that her friends and others do. I do find things out, because she is good friends with my boss's daughter, who tells her parents *everything*. So-and-so is getting 'felt up,' and there are a lot of drugs going on at school. Let me point out that this is middle school, and we are talking about eighth-graders. When I question my daughter with follow-up prompts like 'Do you know anyone who is using drugs?' her answer is always no. If I come right out and say, 'Are you using drugs?' she says 'No way!' I trust her, but I also know how sneaky I was as a teenager, so I get paranoid. I'd feel better if she told me more."

What parent wouldn't? All parents want to be let in on such insider information. Secrets are the currency and essence of your child's friendships. Girls share their secrets with one another. Boys are less likely to tell, but vigilantly protect one another's secrets.

Realistically, the grapevine is how many of us get the dirt on middle schoolers. Questions and confrontations don't usually work. Instead they trigger "I'm not a baby anymore, can't I just go out without a third degree?" "Don't you trust me?"

Mothers, fathers, stepparents, or grandparents responsible for supervision are entitled to certain logistical information.

However, the very same guardians are not entitled to know everything. One New York teenager scrawled in huge letters "Parents don't have a right to know about my friends and my friends' secrets!" You could almost hear her outrage by way of her penmanship. Snooping to learn everything is a violation of your child's right to confidentiality with her peers.

Develop a Privacy Trust

Eavesdropping on telephone calls or pressing your ear to the wall of your child's bedroom door when her friends are over—this is taboo. You won't have to resort to these clandestine ploys when you lay a groundwork that stimulates sharing details about friends and friendship. Develop a privacy trust. By that we mean cultivate a relationship with your middler that honors the inalienable rights of adolescents, including confidentiality, respect, and peer companionship.

Confidentiality. Accept the fact that your child wants it. Remember that confidentiality is not solely a bargain that eleven-year-olds strike up with friends. Your child has unveiled sacred stuff to you, and will continue to do so if you are worthy of that intimacy.

We asked, "What would make you more comfortable sharing your secret side with your parents?" Kids wanted to know that they can trust us, their parents, to keep their secrets.

We interviewed Amy Miron, M.S., and Charles Miron, Ph.D., Maryland, coauthors of *How to Talk to Teens About Love, Relationships & S-E-X*, who told us: "Our clinical experience has taught us to deal with confidentiality. That principle becomes a cornerstone of trust. We believe the same rules apply to privacy. In clinical practice what goes on within the four walls of the office stays within those walls. When a client believes what they are sharing with you is confidential and you breach confidentiality, there is a problem.

"We think there is a direct parallel between the clinical issue of confidentiality and the issue of preteen/teen privacy. Privacy guidelines need to be set by the parents early in their children's lives. If the family starts with the assumption of privacy, the young person should be informed under what conditions a parent will violate it. The parent shouldn't take these issues lightly, as once you breach privacy that has been agreed to, you are sending a loud message of distrust."

Officially tell your child you will honor her need to have secrets with her friends or siblings. Furthermore, let her know you will protect any secrets she shares with you. Live up to your promise. Don't tell other parents her secrets. Outline when suspicions and what kind will make you stricter. Draw the line for your child between risky behaviors, that is, drinking, experimenting with drugs, failing in school, and how these will result in the loss of freedom and even privacy.

Respect. Any working rapport features respect. Adults across the board insist upon teens treating them with respect. How many arguments begin over back talk. Yet, respect is a commodity that must flow both ways. Treat all your child's friends with respect, even the ones you don't like. Expressing your reservations is good, necessary. "It worries me that Jason always seems so angry and sarcastic toward you and your sister." That is quite different from spewing derogatory remarks. "That Jason is a pig."

Once you put a confidential insurance policy in place, and abide by treating your child's friendships carefully, your relationship with your child will have fewer conflicts. Your comments will be more accepted. We can't stress how many studies we have read that insist young adolescents want to be monitored and advised.

- A 2001 *Journal of Research on Adolescence* study found girls' well-being rose when their parents questioned them about their friends and the activities they engaged in with those friends. In other words, diplomatic nagging translated into less drinking, delayed forays into sex, and less depression.
- The Sesame Workshop collected artwork, specifically pictures and writings from children ages six to eleven, and attempted to glean their perspective. The 2001 report, called "A View from the Middle— Life Through the Eyes of Children in Middle Childhood," underscored how children wanted relationships with adults that involved getting guidance on navigating their lives.

We assume that our middlers withhold every morsel about their lives and want to act as free agents in the clandestine company of their buddies without our input. Wrong! Understand that ten- to fifteen-year-olds are schizoid by nature, full of contradictions. They want that unchaperoned private life, and they want our guidance.

Peer companionship Your child's friends are not *the enemy*. Nor are they your *competition*. Ten- to fifteen-year-olds (and beyond) need friends and adults. They don't need adults who act like their friends. Boys and girls need peer friendships in order to explore their feelings, the crises in their lives, and to develop ways to resolve issues and emotions.

Boys and girls go about friendship differently. Girls operate face-to-face seeking comfort, advice, and a sense of connection. Boys operate more side-to-side, tackling activities in which to find a sense of membership, and seeking a place in the pecking order of teenage life. Our children cannot truly find themselves without rambling and roaming around in pairs or packs. That is not to say we have no place in our friends-driven children's lives.

A study by the Girl Scouts Research Institute released in 2000 echoes how indispensable parents are, even as children reach toward outside influences. Among girls eight to nine years old, 91 percent seek out their mothers for advice. These girls felt their moms were the most trusted source of accurate knowledge. Only 52 percent of that sampling looked to their friends for counsel. With slightly older girls, ten- to twelve-year-olds, friends and parents ran neck and neck in the advice game. Peers barely edged Mom out: 77 percent went to friends, 75 percent to Mom.

Too Much Information—
What Do You Do with It?

What happens when you are a thorough, responsible parent and you stumble onto incendiary knowledge? From your child or her brother or sister?

A local newspaper in Chappaqua, New York, decried a *parent-chaperoned* party where young and older adolescents aged fifteen through seventeen drank beer, smoked pot, and watched a stripper in celebration of the high school football season. Parents in the tony community had apparently been wrestling with this "ordinary annual tradition." After the story got out, they wrestled with the scandal as well.

If you had been a parent in that community would you have bucked tradition? Would you have forbidden your jock to attend the party? Hearing about an event like that one poses a real dilemma. Finding one or two good allies could help you and make you more likely to raise objections.

However, a classic parent trap leaves you out on a solitary limb. What happens when your child reveals a secret about a friend, namely that this friend is in trouble. The friend could be depressed, angry and making threats, smoking pot, taking Ecstasy, drinking, having sex.

Your first impulse is probably to heave a sigh of relief. (That is, once you decide this "friend" isn't really your child.) After all, the dangerous state of mind or risky behavior isn't your child's. Then it dawns on you. What do you do with this confidential tidbit? Do you pick up the telephone and call the child-in-question's mother? Or do you discuss what you've heard with the principal at school?

Before you go anywhere with this tale, stop. Focus on your own child. This is more important than anything else. Figure out why your child came to you in the first place. Here are a few possibilities:

Your child is looking for ethical guidance. Let's look at an imaginary scenario. Thirteen-year-old Dakota tells his father that his best friend, Kyle, has started drinking. Maybe Dad is surprised because he knows Kyle comes from a good family. He's met Kyle's parents and knows them to be loving and responsible. Then again, maybe he's not surprised, because Kyle is left home alone often when his parents travel to Kyle's grandmother. She lives out of state and is very ill. His son has invited his eighth-grade friend Kyle to sleep over more than once.

Dakota spills more of the details. He says that Kyle and another boy are draining the liquor cabinet, adding water to the bottles so no one notices a changing level of the brandy and whiskey. Dakota says he refuses to drink with them. However, he's afraid to express his disapproval for fear of looking like a wimp. Dakota doesn't enjoy hanging out and watching his friends get smashed and act like fools, but he is afraid to leave Kyle with this other bad seed. He adds that more and more kids are starting to talk about getting drunk. It's the ticket to being cool.

If your middler finds himself in this situation he is walking a tightrope, and he knows it. On the one hand, he is worried about his friend; on the other he is worried about his reputation. Peer disapproval, appearing to be a goody two-shoes, fitting in, squealing—these are the balls he is trying to juggle without getting clobbered.

Dakota needs help developing defense tactics. Perhaps the first line is coaching him on handling Kyle's invitation. When Kyle wants company at his house, Dakota can say no. He can suggest they meet under his roof instead.

If Dakota does find himself at Kyle's and the drinking starts prepare Kyle by role-playing comebacks. For example, "My parents would ground me for a year if they smelled liquor and they always hug me to check." Or "I'm saving up to buy myself a car and my parents will match my money. If I get caught drinking, the deal is off."

Your child is seeking approval for doing the right thing. Out-of-state soccer tournaments are popular in many communities. Such trips posed a problem for Shelby. Her teammates loved staying in the motel, ordering pizzas, swimming in the motel pool, calling one another on the telephone from room to room, and checking out the boys' soccer teams staying at the motel. Sounds like fun. It surely was, up until after midnight. Shelby told her mom that the coach insisted the girls go to bed at midnight, considering the purpose of the trip—to play and win.

The girls had other ideas. They had convinced their parents to let them bunk together. Several tried to sneak out of their rooms just for the fun of it. In Shelby's room they made a pact; the first one to fall asleep got doused with shaving cream. Shelby decided to return to her parents' room. She needed rest if she was going to be able to play well and not get injured. She got teased by her teammates.

At first, you might think that Shelby's tattling was a round-about way of giving her mother license to tell the coach. Then he would punish the offenders. Not so fast. Shelby swore her mom to secrecy.

When your child reports that others are disobeying rules or not living up to expectations, what she may be looking for is simple: your approval. Doing the right thing doesn't always guarantee a pat on the back from peers. Unfortunately, it's usually just the opposite. A child who takes a coach's pregame instructions seriously is a wet blanket. What Shelby needs is praise for doing the right thing. Tell her she's admirable. You need to add, too, that doing the right thing doesn't always win friends and influence people. Sometimes the reward comes from inside. This is the definition of integrity. Your child is looking for you to underline why she should follow a personal honor code.

Your child is cleverly launching a distraction. Beware the child who is always telling tales painting herself as the only one who is sidestepping mischief. Little Ms. Innocent may have a sophisticated game plan.

Meet Delia, who could charm anyone. Everyone who knew Delia agreed that she topped the social hierarchy in ninth grade. An outgoing personality and smooth social finesse outdid her ample physical attributes. Delia loved telling her parents all the dirt about the soap opera that school had become. Nearly every Monday afternoon, she'd come through the door with "Mom, you wouldn't believe what so-and-so did!" Then she'd follow with the details of who had starting smoking cigarettes, who cheated on the science quiz, who had oral sex for the first time. The more aghast her mother became at the misbehavior of sweet little Ashley from second grade or whomever, the better Delia liked it.

A method to Delia's madness existed. She figured the more secrets she told her mother, the more convinced her mother would be that Delia would never lie. Her mother proudly broadcast, "Delia tells me everything!" Delia smirked in her room thinking to herself, *Yeah I tell her everything about everybody so she thinks that I'd never do any of that daring stuff.* Meanwhile Delia has been experimenting with sexual activity herself, moving from one boy to another in her class She already had a plan if anyone said anything to her mother. She'd just say the ratfink girl was lying, jealous of Delia's popularity.

Over the years talking to experts, parents, and young adolescents, we've learned that middlers behave according to the mores of their friends. In other words, if all your child's friends smoke cigarettes or drink, your child is probably doing it, too. If your child is forever tattling tales, chances are she is trying to throw you off her own risky business.

Your child needs help processing his emotions. Dan seemed troubled to his mother. After school he retreated to his room and didn't say much. Then one evening after a bit of parental probing, Dan confessed he was really worried about his best friend, Mike. He explained that Mike was no longer any fun. Mike didn't smile or joke anymore. Always a quiet boy, now Mike seemed even more quiet. Dan said he was sick and tired of trying to cheer his friend up. Dan said he had a theory that Mike was really angry inside about something, but what? Dan didn't have a clue and he didn't think that Mike did either. Dan confided he felt so frustrated. He'd begun avoiding Mike, but that just makes him feel worse.

Young adolescents are very emotional. They are in the midst of an enormous growth spurt. They are experiencing strong feelings courtesy of hormones with which they are totally unfamiliar. Middlers like Dan and Mike feel intensely. Yet they aren't always sure what name goes along with what feeling. Guilt. Disappointment. Anger. Frustration. The feelings can weigh heavily. Middlers may not know what to do or where to go with these feelings.

At first solving the mystery of Mike's funk seems like the issue. However, the real issue here is Dan and his experience. Dan is feeling too much pressure, feeling responsible for someone else's emotional state.

If your child confides to you secret information about a friend's anger or sadness, he is looking for help for himself. He may want to get himself off the hook and find someone else to resolve the friend's turmoil. You need to let your child know that he is not responsible for solving another child's problem. The truth is he couldn't reverse a friend's melancholy or rage even if he wanted to. What your child can learn to do is face his feelings and define what his role and responsibility are in the situation. For example, Dan could confront Mike with something like this:

"You seem so down. You really should talk to someone. Have you told your parents? How about taking aside the coach or the school counselor? I miss the fun friend you used to be. You don't have to stay all bottled up like this."

Then reassure your child that he has done everything he

can do. He can't fix people or things. His job is to focus on his emotions and learn to work through them.

As you can see from these typical confessionals, sometimes adolescents are bursting with information. They are up to or in need of something. It could be free reign to dabble in danger, or reassurance. It's your job to read between the lines of too much information.

Taking the Accusation Further

Suppose you've analyzed the situation and given your child exactly what he needs but you have the nagging feeling you need to pass along the information. Your buttinsky urge should be measured against how serious the secret is. If the information goes to a child's safety or well-being, for example, involves suicide or any threat of violence, then you need to go to someone. Explain to your child why you must violate his trust in this instance.

We asked teachers if they would violate a confidence, pass along a student's secret. "I'd pass along the confidence from my student only with the child's permission or if the situation posed real danger," offered a teacher from New York. Many agreed.

Be prepared for the reaction of the offending child's parents, though. Most fit into one of these categories.

- *Thanks for sharing that.* This is the optimal reaction. It's also the rarest.
- *Where's your proof?* Many parents today cannot accept criticism of their children. If you don't think

the parent takes the risk seriously, then look to a
school counselor or official to take the next step.
That's all you can do.

- Denial that goes like this: *"Your kid doesn't like my
kid."* Butt out. Don't let your good intentions de-
scend into a he said/she said ongoing rebuttal.
- Remember, your main job here is to ensure the
safety of your child. You can try to be your brother's
keeper, but you can rarely do this alone without the
cooperation of the other child's parents.

The friendship zone is a challenge for parents since young adolescents are knee-deep in a secret society. Maintaining that advice edge and keeping connected to a child is feasible. Hearing
secrets does happen. Your odds improve when you act dis-
creetly and tread delicately in the friendship department. To let
your insecurity lead you into breaching matters of confidentiality will alienate and jeopardize your child during these years.
Yes, once upon a time you were your baby boy's best friend,
your little girl's favorite playmate. Now you have been replaced.
Rest assured: you are still his and her most significant ally.

What You Should Do

Respect your child's need to have friends, to share
    secrets, and to be a friend.
Monitor your child's social comings and goings.
Evaluate her friends and make calm, probing comments.
Weigh a child's confidences to see when she needs advice.

What You Should Not Do

Regard her friends as the enemy.
Ignore disturbing signs of a child's covering-up behavior.
Criticize her friends.
Jump to conclusions of guilt when a child confesses a
    secret mistake a friend has made.

Chapter 4

The Internet

"g2g pir" ("Got to go. Parent in room.")

SmaToG86: u goin 2 the party this Friday?
GJB5874: yea u?
SmaToG86: yeah ur goin w/ash right?
GJB5874: yup u goin w/nel?
SmaToG86: nah im goin stag
GJB5874: y dont u go w/paul? he talks bout u alot
SmaToG86: ugh he does?
GJB5874: yea y the ugh
SmaToG86: cuz he freaks me out
GJB5874: oic
SmaToG86: neway . . . pir

It's not your imagination. You and your young adolescent speak a different language. Middlers use shortland for talking in cyberspace. Abbreviations and dropped punctuation help conversations move at lightning speed. But young adolescents have another reason for typing in code. Many hope that the jumble of letters and numbers will confuse prying parents who try to get a glimpse of the screen.

Most exchanges are G-rated and friendly. In the above conversation between Greg and Tara, they talk about their mutual friend, Ashley, and an upcoming party. (A full glossary of commonly used abbreviations is included on page 140.) But the alphabet soup may make you suspicious. Like most parents, you probably worry about on-line chatting. Whom is your child talking to? What is being said? Is it safe? Should you monitor every word (even if you don't understand most of what flashes across the screen)?

In this chapter we will break the code of young adolescent chatter on the Internet. We will sort through the technical terms so that you will find the Internet less intimidating. There are dangers, to be sure. You will see what those hazards are and learn how you can help your child steer clear. Yet the vast majority of middlers don't use the Internet to download pornography or meet strangers. They use this electronic medium the way their parents used the telephone, to talk with their friends. Our guidelines will help you set reasonable boundaries so that the Internet can play a role in your child's life without overtaking it.

You should have more than a general idea of where your child goes on the Internet. But staying on top of the situation 24/7 is impossible. The best way for you to protect your young adolescent in cyberspace is to make sure that your child understands the rules and the dangers. That way, when he is on his own, he will know how to spot trouble and how to react. Giving him these safety tools will give you peace of mind. In this chapter, we will show you what to do to accomplish that goal.

The Internet has opened up new vistas for our children. While you may be less confident in cyberspace than your child is, you don't need computer expertise to teach values. Your guidance and sensitivity is the software your child needs now.

From the Military to the Mainstream

Parents remember a time when the Internet didn't exist. For most ten- to fifteen-year-olds, however, the Internet has always been an important part of their lives, both academically and so-cially. In fact, the Internet only opened to the public in 1992. "The Internet began as a military experiment," according to William F. Moylan, a member of the U.S. Secret Service's Electronic Crimes Task Force. "Could we continue to commu-nicate around destroyed areas?" To find an answer, the military funded the development of supercomputers, locating them in colleges and other academic centers around the country. This early network began in 1969, and while primitive compared with the speed and services now available, succeeded in its goal—to link up users from one place to another with a wire cable.

"E-mail became popular almost immediately," Moylan says. Colleges paid people to test whether the system could handle a large flow of traffic. Those who used e-mail became addicted and kept their addresses even after leaving academia. That helped bring nonacademics into the network. The World Wide Web, the electronic pages that present information on the Internet, came into being in 1994.

According to a 2001 survey from Teenage Research Unlimited, 78 percent of teens spend six hours on-line each week. That figure compares to 97 percent of teens who say they watch ten hours of television each week, 91 percent who spend six hours talking on a regular phone weekly, 58 percent who spend four hours a week reading for pleasure, and 50 percent who spend three hours a week on homework. With the various technologies converging—listening to music and watching video on-line—teens will soon spend more time in front of their computer screens than anywhere else. Parents reluctant to deal with the Internet have no choice: Pandora's Box is open.

Many parents understand the dangers that exist on the Internet. There is a huge gap, however, between what parents say and what children hear.

In 2001, the Pew Internet and American Life Project dramatically revealed this communication gap. This organization conducted phone interviews with 754 youths between the ages of twelve and seventeen and their parents. Here are some of the discrepancies the study unveiled:

Sixty-one percent of the parents claimed to have rules governing Internet use, but only 37 percent of the young people said they were subjected to any such rules.

Similarly, 61 percent of parents said they routinely checked to see where their children had ventured on-line. Only 27 percent of teens said they had been so monitored.

Sixty-eight percent of parents reported they sat with their children while they were on-line. Yet only 48 percent of the children said that occurred.

If you have avoided learning about the Internet, now is the

time to do so. There are many ways to communicate on-line. Knowing what these ways are and how to avoid dangers can help you keep your young adolescent safe.

Getting to Know Your Way Around

Think of the World Wide Web as a large city, crisscrossed with many highways, avenues, and side streets. Within the city limits, there are fascinating places to visit—shopping malls, movie theaters, jazz clubs, parks, museums, libraries, and schools. Like any metropolis, however, seedy areas exist. Anyone looking for danger can find it—pornographic shops, adult sex parlors, stores carrying lewd magazines and toys. And cruising through the Web is just like walking down a city street. If a stranger stops you and asks for personal information—your name, address, phone number—you would refuse. Feel threatened? You would run for your life and flag down the nearest police officer. Why should it be any different on the Web?

Young adolescents are, by their nature, open and trusting. They often don't have the social maturity and experience that make adults wary. Familiarize yourself with the details of the Internet, where problems are likely to occur, and how these traps can be avoided. You will be better equipped to advise your child. Here are some things you need to know about:

Screen Names

In cyberspace, your screen name becomes your identity. Typically, this moniker serves as your e-mail address and the name you use in a chat room. Young adolescents are creative with their screen names, revealing a bit of themselves, a favorite hobby, sport, pet, nickname, or physical characteristic. While you don't want to stifle your child's imagination, make sure her screen name doesn't provide ammunition for someone determined to take advantage of her trust. In cyberspace, bonds are easily created. Say your child's screen name reveals her to be a soccer player, goalie123, for example. Here's a conversation that could happen:

dynamo2: goalie? u play soccr or hockey?
goalie123: sccr
dynamo2: me2 ima sweeper
goalie123: cool
dynamo2: what team?
goalie123: riverside we r undefeated
dynamo2: my team sucks 3–0 what's yr jersey #?
goalie123: lucky 13

This young adolescent knows not to give out her name or address. But in her enthusiasm to discuss soccer, she let down her guard and gave out her school and jersey number. If dynamo2 wants to target her, he has clues to locate her. In fact, undercover police officers conducting a sting operation to ferret out cyber predators found that the screen name soccerboy13 attracted unpleasant on-line advances.

Precocious teens often use screen names that are flirtatious. Christina Long, thirteen, a sixth-grade cheerleader at a Catholic school in Danbury, Connecticut, used the screen name LongToohot4u. After exchanging e-mails with a twenty-five-year-old man from Greenwich, she apparently met him several times and they had sex. When she failed to return from the mall one night, her aunt reported her missing. Her body was found along a secluded road. Police said she had been strangled and her Internet "date" was arrested and charged with strangling her. After Christina's death, police uncovered her secret life of cruising the Internet to meet men.

Learn your child's screen name and limit her to one. With a service like America Online, you begin with a master screen name but can create up to six additional screen names, each with its own e-mail address. However, only the person with the master screen name can add additional ones. Make sure you control the master screen name, thus making it impossible for your child to add other on-line identities. If you don't use AOL, check to see how screen names are handled with your ISP (Internet Service Provider). The Pew study uncovered subterfuge by many young people. Fifty-nine percent said they have more than one screen name and 24 percent admitted to keeping one identity secret for use when they want to go on-line incognito. Hiding behind a false identity is like making an anonymous phone call. Make sure your child understands that you do not endorse such behavior.

Password

On-line, your password is the key that unlocks the door to cyberspace. Once you type in your password, you assume your screen name and have access to e-mail, chat rooms, and the World Wide Web. Middlers often do not guard their passwords carefully enough. One mother tells this story: "My daughter gave out her password to a friend. Unfortunately, her friend used that information to sign on and pose as my daughter. Nothing serious happened. The girl just wanted to find out if a boy liked her. But my daughter was shaken by the incident and now changes her password regularly."

E-mail

Hands down, e-mail is the most popular function for the Internet and one our kids have eagerly embraced. Middlers use e-mail not only to exchange greetings but to send pictures, jokes, and links to interesting Web sites.

E-mail is different from "snail mail," paper envelopes delivered by the U.S. Postal Service. While your middler receives few letters each day, he may receive dozens of e-mails. You can tell a letter by its envelope—whether it's from a personal friend, magazine solicitation, or correspondence from school. With e-mail, the description may give little or no information as to what the actual missive contains.

Few middlers, indeed, few adults, understand that e-mails, unlike paper mail, are not private communication. An e-mail sent to one friend could easily be forwarded to hundreds of others. Deleting an e-mail does not necessarily destroy it. (Not like burning a letter.) The message still lives on hard drives and can be recovered in the future. While middlers are inclined to pour out their hearts in e-mail messages, make sure your daughter knows that her most private thoughts could be made very public.

You probably would never read your child's personal letters

or diary. But because you know less about who is sending him e-mails, you might be tempted to invade his privacy. Your desire to protect your child is sound. Yet reading his personal communications could destroy the trust between you. "My mom has a detective program so she can read my e-mail and check my instant messages and see every site I visit," says one boy. "How does this make me feel? Not good."

If you decide you do want to see all of your child's e-mails, the best way to manage that is to share a screen name. However, that might mean your child would also see your communications, something you may not want to happen. Because middlers receive a large volume of e-mails daily, you might have trouble finding your own amid this onslaught.

Suppose you allow your son to have his own screen name but still insist on reading all of his correspondence? You would still face the daunting task of plowing through all those e-mails, many of them written in middler code. Do you really have the time and energy to devote to this task daily?

One mother believes her child set a Guinness Record with four hundred in one day. Also, middlers can now exchange e-mails, called text messages, using their cell phones, either phone to phone or phone to computer. One mother reports that her teenage son exchanged 320 text messages with his friends in one month! Add that number to the hundreds of e-mails this boy is also receiving, and a parent would have to make this monitoring job a full-time one to stay on top.

A better way to go is to give your child his own e-mail address after telling him your expectations. He should never send or receive an e-mail from an unknown source. Show him how to delete an e-mail (if he doesn't already know) before he opens it. Many viruses are activated when an e-mail from a suspicious source is opened. Often the come-on line makes the e-mail irresistible. "You have won money!" or "Free tickets to the upcoming concert!" In the event your child opens an e-mail that contains objectionable language, threats, or anything that makes him feel uncomfortable, he should tell you immediately.

Web Sites

Think of a Web site as you would a magazine. The opening page, or home page, is like the magazine's cover with a table of contents. Click on an item and zoom through additional pages. At some sites, you will find much to explore, most of it useful, safe, and fun. But the World Wide Web has its dark side—pornography. Experts say there are forty thousand pornographic Web sites already up, with no end in sight. These sites attract lots of visitors, 17.5 million a month, according to Nielsen NetRatings. These sites are big business, producing close to three billion dollars in revenue in 2003, according to the research firm Datamonitor. Some pornographers mask the true nature of their Web sites by using child-friendly names like Barbie, Disney, or ESPN. Middlers wander onto such sites accidentally. "One time I was looking up information and something gross popped up," says a thirteen-year-old girl. "I exited out."

Some young adolescents purposefully enter these X-rated sites. Why? "To find out stuff I don't want to ask my parents," says one thirteen-year-old girl. Another thirteen-year-old adds: "Because I can learn things."

If you find out your child has visited a pornographic Web site, don't overreact. She may have gone there by mistake. Or, he may have questions about sex that he is embarrassed to ask you. In days past, young adolescent boys hid copies of *Playboy* under their mattresses, safe from the eyes of prying parents. Perhaps you need to have more talks about sex with your child. His foray onto a pornographic Web site may give you the opportunity you need to open a discussion. Talk with your child to find out what happened before jumping to conclusions and meting out punishment.

Don't overlook the harmful nature of these Web sites, however. Some of the material is hard-core, way beyond anything you would find in an adult magazine sold on a newsstand. And a popular theme is the sexual use and abuse of young children. While most of these sites have a portal where you need to type in a credit card number to enter, others allow a peek before you need to pay anything. A young adolescent who habitually visits such sites is courting danger. At a time when your child is attempting to figure out his sexuality, exposure to the warped world of pornography can only be damaging. Women, for example, are often treated cruelly, as sex objects, on these Web sites, certainly not the message you hope your son or daughter will learn.

Besides warning your child about these Web sites, keep a dialogue going about sex, a topic many parents work to avoid. Your child should know that he can ask you anything and confide in you. Some young adolescents who worry about being gay are afraid to discuss this topic with their parents. Going to Web sites where these topics are openly discussed is less threatening, helps to ease their anxiety, and opens up a world of people with similar sexual leanings. You can see where this is going, however. Those on-line relationships can easily lead to a face-to-face meeting where your child could be at serious risk of be-ing harmed. Let your child know that he can talk with you about anything—*anything*—and follow through.

Unwanted E-mails

Because young adolescents visit so many Web sites, their e-mail addresses end up on marketer lists. Your child each day proba-bly receives a ton of unsolicited e-mails, called "spam." Some of these messages are annoying but harmless. These are often come-ons to buy something, from CDs and DVDs to teeth-whitening kits and weight-loss programs. The tag line smartly uses your child's name to give it a personal touch. "Jeremy, You May Have Won!" Such a missive can be irresistible to open. Other e-mails are more sinister. "I get two hundred e-mails a day, but a lot of them are to buy things," says one seventh-grade boy. "Sometimes they are about pornography. I got one the other day, 'Hot teens having sex with dogs.' I deleted it." A child who unwittingly opens such an e-mail may be traumatized.

The Children's Online Privacy Protection Act (COPPA) safeguards the on-line privacy of young children. This law re-quires certain commercial Web sites to get permission from parents before collecting, using, or disclosing personal infor-mation from children under the age of thirteen. Many of these Web sites and on-line services feature animated characters and obviously are aimed at a younger audience. Typically, a child must ask for a parent's permission before he would be allowed to fill out personal information. Perhaps you have received e-mails from such sites in the past after your child paid a visit and asked you to give your consent.

COPPA's main purpose is to shield children from the zealousness of marketers. But this law has its limits. Children, especially savvy young adolescents, can skirt the parental approval form by typing in an older age. And, of course, there are Web sites that do not come under the jurisdiction of COPPA because their pages are not aimed at young children. If your child visits some of these, he is sure to receive unwanted e-mails.

While you may not want to read your child's correspondence, you might ask him to call up his mail to read the headings. If you see anything alarming, investigate further. Your ISP can help you set parameters for receiving e-mail, thus eliminating some spam. You will need to remain vigilant, however, checking in occasionally with your child about his e-mail.

Chat Rooms

To a middler, chatting often involves sending messages back and forth between classmates, similar to talking on the phone. Parents hear the word *chat,* however, and automatically picture a cyber chat room where pedophiles lurk. All chat, therefore, becomes suspect.

Middlers like to talk, so it's no surprise that they embrace chatting on-line. Chat rooms are like party lines in cyberspace. Groups of people, usually those interested in a specific topic, gather to pass the time and share information. You've probably been to a chat room yourself. As parenting authors, we chat with parents about our books. Chats can be informative and enjoyable.

Chats, however, can lead to danger. Adults with criminal

intent roam through chat rooms looking for victims. David Finkelhor and his associates from the Crimes Against Children Research Center at the University of New Hampshire interviewed 1,501 adolescents, ages ten to seventeen, who use the Internet regularly and detailed the findings in *Online Victimization: A Report on the Nation's Youth*. According to the survey results, one in five kids received a sexual solicitation approach over the Internet during the year. One in thirty-three received an aggressive sexual solicitation. In other words, someone asked to meet them somewhere, called them on the telephone, or sent them regular mail, money, or gifts. Only about one-fourth of those approached told a parent.

How are young adolescents approached? When chatting in cyberspace, anyone can create a false identity. To facilitate a meeting, the predator focuses on a chat in his geographical area. He assumes an identity and lurks in the chat room for long stretches, listening and biding his time. Soon, he selects his victim—let's call her Jennifer—and begins to gather information. He learns that Jennifer is an only child whose mother died a year ago. She is being raised by her father, who is now dating a younger woman. Jennifer is feeling alone and scared.

"If a parent and a child don't have a great relationship, the child will seek attention elsewhere," says Marianna Novielli, an information research analyst who works with Moylan at the U.S. Secret Service.

Jennifer seeks that attention on-line. She visits a chat room for teens and talks about her home life. She mentions that she loves cats and her only companion these days is her tabby, Snickers. Her dream, she tells others in the chat room, is to move to a big city and design clothing that will sell in the most prestigious stores. She loves to pore over fashion magazines and sketch her own designs.

The stalker now has plenty of data on Jennifer and he is ready to move in. He enters the chat room with a new screen name and begins talking. He identifies himself as a teenage boy who recently lost his father. His mom is dating a man he hates and he is thinking of running away. Of course, he would take his only friend, his dog, Jumpers. His destination? A big city where he can maybe get work as a model.

Jennifer can't believe what she is seeing on the screen. It's too good to be true. She's found her soul mate. Soon, she and the stalker have moved out of the chat room, chatting privately, then sending e-mails. Jennifer gives him her phone number and they talk several times. She is totally won over. Here is someone who truly understands how she feels because he feels that way, too. When he suggests a meeting, she is only too eager to comply. She can't wait to meet this boy. She agrees not to tell anyone where she is going. "That's part of the seduction, not telling anyone," says Moylan.

Of course, when the meeting comes off, Jennifer discovers that her Romeo is not who she thought he was. "Sexual predators range from a thirty-something unmarried man living at home with his mother, to a married man with a wife, family, a good job, someone who is upstanding in his community," says Novielli. Finkelhor's study found, however, that the perpetrator is more likely to be an older teen or young adult between the ages of eighteen and twenty-five. In other words, young people are often approached by their peers and asked to engage in or provide sexual information. That fact is chilling, because a peer will relate more easily to someone his own age and who can be more persuasive.

Whatever the age of Jennifer's stalker, he is not interested in helping her; he wants to hurt her. She may be raped, tortured, kidnapped, or killed. Because she did not tell anyone whom she was meeting or where she was going, her father has little to tell the police. Even if her father suspected she was the victim of a cybercrime, the police would have difficulty tracking whom she talked to. "Unless they are logged (saved), live chats are difficult to re-create afterward," says Moylan.

Some parents outlaw chats. Others allow chats with boundaries—certain chats, for example, or chatting only when a parent is present. Whatever decision you make, help your child understand your reasoning. In the cyberspace chat, nothing is what it seems. Visit a chat room with her and demonstrate how easily you can fool others into thinking you are a teenager. Get her to question what is being said on-line so that she will be cautious. "I only visited a chat room a few times and I told my parents," says a twelve-year-old girl. Stress that she won't be punished if she runs into a problem as long as she tells you.

Private Chats

It's possible to arrange a private chat on-line with AOL by naming a chat and inviting friends to join in. Because you need to know the name of the chat to get into the room, these chats are usually okay.

Instant Messaging

Among the functions of the Internet, instant messaging (IM) is coming close to replacing the telephone as the number one way to reach out and touch someone. According to the Pew survey, close to thirteen million teenagers use IM, with 69 percent saying they use it at least several times a week. When you IM someone, a special dialogue screen pops up. Only two people can IM each other back and forth, but many young adolescents are adept at carrying on more than one IM conversation at a time.

Middlers, for the most part, use the instant message feature with their friends. But every now and then, a stranger who has seen your child's screen name on-line will attempt to begin a conversation. Make sure your child knows not to respond to IMs from unfamiliar screen names. This method is another one used by pedophiles to make contact with victims.

It's possible to block IMs from people you and your child do not know by changing certain settings once you are on-line. Do so if that will give you peace of mind about who can contact your child.

Discuss with your child the best ways to use instant messaging properly. In the Pew Survey, 37 percent of teens admitted they used IM to write something to a friend they would not have said in person. Seventeen percent used IM to ask someone out, while 13 percent hid behind the electronic screen to break up. While using IM might embolden a shy Romeo to ask out a girl, "dumping" her electronically might lead to hurt feelings and reputations.

Profiles and Personal Web Pages

Your child can create a profile or personal Web page to tell others about herself. Some of these profiles and Web pages are creative and funny. You can see the danger, however, in putting out on public display personal information that a stalker can use to his benefit. If your child wants to launch himself into cyberspace this way, ask what he plans to include. Tell him your concerns and ask to see what he has written.

Young adolescents can use Web pages to humiliate and bully other children. Moylan says his office often receives complaints when children are harassed in this manner. He says that tormentors can create a Web page where a child's photograph will be distorted, "morphed," in a way to make her ugly. A common caption is "For a good time call. . . ." This type of teasing is not new. How many parents can remember seeing such statements scribbled on bathroom walls? But with the advent of the Internet, these put-downs can reach a much wider audience. Your child needs to understand the hurtful nature of such actions. According to Moylan, such harassment is a misdemeanor and can land your child in legal hot water. If your child is on the receiving end of this abuse, make a report to the school and the authorities.

Favorite Places

The Internet has a dark side, to be sure. But there are far more positive sites for your child to explore. Here are some suggestions:

AOL Teens has sites that feature music artists, current movies, fashion trends, and a way to get help with homework.

Neopets is a virtual pet site where your child can adopt a virtual pet, play games, and trade greetings with other pet owners, some thirty million around the world. It's free and parental permission is required before your child can participate. "I love neopets!" one twelve-year-old girl told us in our survey.

The Federal Consumer Information Center runs sites for kids and teens, www.kids.gov and www.teens.gov. There are links for other sites—everything from careers, government, fighting crime, and money, to music, plants and animals, and recreation. Click on fun stuff, for example, and your child can get free army posters or learn more about the Peace Corps in a global virtual tour.

The Scholastic Web site (www.scholastic.com) includes a link to Harry Potter, where your child can play games and interact with the characters.

A young adolescent's curiosity and sense of adventure often take him to places you would never discover on your own, sites that could be fun to explore together. Make time to travel through cyberspace together. Review your child's favorite places. You will discover a hidden side of your child, one that will impress and excite you. Cyberspace doesn't have to be a den of iniquity. Let your child show you the way.

Younger children may be curious about Web sites visited by an older sibling. If your children share a computer, favorite places that are okay for an older teen (some music sites for rock groups, for example), may be too edgy for a young adolescent. Talk with your children about keeping site visits age-appropriate.

Sites at School

Most schools now operate their own Web sites. What is on these sites and how they are used varies according to the school. Educators are sensitive to privacy issues and tend to limit the personal information posted about individual students. Sometimes, however, private data may be released with the best intentions. If your child is the school's star basketball player, for example, you may not object to having the school post his name, jersey number, and photo on the site, typical data that would appear in a newspaper article. You might object, however, to having released his address, e-mail address, or other personal details not related to his sport. Remember, any information that can be accessed by the public—and school Web sites generally can be—may make your child a target. Visit your child's school's Web site now and then to review the information. If there is anything there that makes you uncomfortable, tell the school.

The Web at School

At the beginning of each year, you and your child may sign a contract promising that the child will comply with the proper use of the Internet at school. Then, you hear nothing else about the Internet from the teachers for the rest of the year. Should you be concerned?

According to Moylan, you should be. "I don't know if teachers are any more clued in than other adults, he says. "Schools were in a mad rush to get their children on the Internet, afraid that they would fall behind in the technology race." Too often, however, teachers were not as knowledgeable as the children. "It used to be that the teachers disappeared and let the kids go on without being supervised," Moylan says. Now, because schools can be held liable if anything happens, times are changing.

In our survey, schools cited filtering software, close supervision of passwords, and monitoring by teachers as the most common safety measures used. "I am with them in the lab and constantly supervising," says one teacher. Another adds: "I monitor students' activities on the Internet by watching what sites they are visiting. Also, our school has filtering software installed."

But this safety net still has gaping holes. "I only allow use when they are supervised in my class," says a technology teacher. However, he admits: "I do not track them when they are in the library or other places." Some schools have curtailed filtering software because certain programs also block sites that are legitimate. Because the word *breast*, for example, is on the list of unacceptable terms to scan for, a student doing research on breast cancer would not be able to access appropriate information. Doing away with these firewalls, however, means teachers must be even more vigilant.

At the next parent night, ask for a more detailed explanation of what goes on in the school's computer lab. Some schools hold technology nights where you can learn more about the Internet, and ask questions about school policy. This session is important enough for you to take the time to attend.

In addition, talk with your child's technology teacher. What is said in the classroom can help to reinforce what you are trying to do at home. If children understand the dangers of wandering around on-line, and are lectured about the proper use of cyberspace, they are more likely to adopt that behavior at home, too.

Photos

Sending photos over the Internet can be a great way to keep in touch with relatives and friends near and far. Sending photos to complete strangers, however, can quickly lead to trouble. Talk with your child about the dangers. An on-line predator could send her photo to others and she could wind up with her picture on an objectionable Web site. Tell her she should check with you before sending any pictures anywhere on the Web.

High-Speed Access

Now that the Internet can be accessed through cable wires or high-speed telephone wires that won't tie up the phone lines, it may be more difficult for you to monitor how long your child stays on-line. One father remarks: "When the Internet tied up our phone line, I knew as soon as the phone stopped ringing at night that my son was on-line. I could remind him about time limits."

Don't lose track of the time your child is on-line. While your middler may moan that you are ruining his social life, remind him that all activities should be enjoyed in moderation. If you like, set a time limit for Internet use. Better yet, encourage him to use the Internet with a purpose—to check e-mail, do homework, play a game—then sign off. With high-speed access, your child can remain on-line indefinitely with no cost to you. But the cost to him could be high.

Cover-ups—
How to Spot Trouble

You won't be able to watch your child every minute she is on-line nor should you want to. What you can do, however, is to talk with her frequently about her on-line adventures, where she goes, whom she talks with. Don't be afraid to ask direct questions:

"Has anyone on-line used vulgar language?"

"What would you do if someone asked you your real name? Has that happened?"

"Did you ever talk to anyone you don't know? How did you meet this person?"

"Has anyone ever asked you to meet in person?"

Role-play with your daughter so she knows what she should do if someone on-line makes her feel uncomfortable. If anyone harasses your child on the Web or sends her messages or images that are obscene, lewd, filthy, or indecent, you can report it to your ISP and the National Center for Missing & Exploited Children's CyberTipline at www.cybertipline.com or by calling 1-800-843-5678.

Certain children are more inclined to seek out comfort and companionship on the Internet. The typical profile is one of a child who is lonely, depressed, unattractive (or thinks she's unattractive), and lacking self-confidence to deal with people face-to-face. Young adolescents in general are worried about whether they are appealing to the opposite sex. Most young people, however, find someone they can trust within their own circle to confide in. The perfect victim is a middler who is obsessed with his sexuality and feels isolated. Young adolescent boys who are troubled about being gay are vulnerable to on-line predators who feed into those anxieties. While it may seem cathartic to talk with someone on-line, there is too great a chance that a young adolescent will stumble into a situation he cannot handle.

Your innocent child may wander onto an X-rated Web site or go into a questionable chat room out of curiosity. "I have gone into chat rooms to see what's going on," admits one thirteen-year-old girl. Another young teen told our survey: "It's fun and they aren't that bad." However, one twelve-year-old boy reveals he went to "weird chat rooms," and ends his comments with, "I don't want to tell you."

Once your child enters this world, however, her life may never be the same. At the least she may find what she saw disturbing and those memories may influence how she feels about her sexuality. At the worst, she may continue to visit, risking disaster with every on-line visit.

That's what happened to Katherine Tarbox, whose book, *Katie.com, My Story*, tells a harrowing tale of what can happen when trusting teenagers venture into the brutal world of cybersex. Katie, who lived in New Canaan, Connecticut, and felt abandoned by her workaholic mother and aloof stepfather, sought companionship on-line. In a chat room, she met "Mark," who described himself as a twenty-three-year-old Californian. He seemed warm, sensitive, caring, and filled Katie's need for someone who could understand and love her. While on a trip with her swim team in Texas, Katie agreed to meet Mark in his hotel room. He traveled to Texas to meet Katie. Mark turned out to be Frank Kufrovich, forty-one, who had a history of luring young people into meetings where he pressured them into having sex. Katie was rescued from Frank's hotel room when her mother, accompanying the team as a chaperone and staying in the same hotel, was worried about her daughter and tracked her to the predator's room. For several years afterward, Katie's world was turned upside down as her case against Frank proceeded in court while her personal life was derailed. Her book makes worthwhile reading.

Besides talking to your child, keep a watchful eye. Your child's behavior may change because of his transgressions in cyberspace. Here are some warning signs to look out for:

Changes in your child's sleep patterns. Also, disturbing dreams, even bedwetting.

Acting out at school. This behavior is more likely in a boy. Girls may become depressed and withdrawn.

Use of inappropriate language, particularly language of a sexual nature.

Mention of adults you don't know and vague explanations of how your child knows these people.

Too much time spent on the Internet, particularly late at night.

Frequent downloading of files. Watch those that end in .gif or .jpg. These files could contain pornographic images.

Hiding computer disks. If your child is downloading pornographic files, he may put them on disks so that

you won't see them on your hard drive, or he may be
taking them to school to share with friends.

Charges on your credit card statements that you can't ac-
count for. Watch for those that merely identify themselves as "Web sites."

Keep in touch with other parents. You may feel secure about
your child's on-line use when she is under your roof. What does
she do at her friends' homes? With AOL and other ISPs, you
don't have to be on your home computer to sign on to the
Internet with your own screen name. Your daughter may have
a cyberlife away from home.

Taboo Invasions—
Moves That Can Alienate Your Child

You know the risks and you want to protect your child.
Obviously, the stakes are high. Yet the Internet is a valuable
informational tool, one that can serve your child well in the
years ahead. Come up with a plan that will allow your child
the independence she needs to explore and make some decisions on her own, while preserving your own peace of mind.
Remember that you know your child best; get to know the
Internet, too. Better yet, get to know what your child likes to
do and is likely to do on the Internet. Then you can make a
plan.

Unless you have serious reasons for concern (past transgressions, for example) try to avoid using filtering software to
rein in your young adolescent. Why? For several reasons:

You send a powerful message that you don't trust your child. While you may tell your child you are just trying to protect him from pedophiles, he's smarter than that. He knows you don't trust him to follow your rules. Unless he gives you a reason to doubt him, start him out by laying out your expectations without restricting his movements.

You may send him elsewhere. Your child may go to a friend's house to freely roam on the Internet. You will not be able to monitor him.

You may unfairly prevent your child from social interaction with her friends. One mother tells this tale: "We installed AOL on my twelve-year-old daughter's new computer. I was worried about the Internet, so we installed a filtering program. She seemed okay with that restriction in the beginning. But soon she discovered that she couldn't IM any of her friends and even had trouble doing research for school on-line. We had many arguments before I realized that she wasn't fighting to go into pornographic chat rooms. She really just wanted to talk with her friends. We removed the software and haven't had a problem since."

You may be outgunned. A determined young adolescent will get around anything you put in place to establish cyber boundaries. "My parents snoop, so I'm learning to hack," says one boy. Another adds: "I've seen my parents snoop around my computer. But I password-protect everything."

Too Much Information— Reading E-mail

Think back to some of the notes you passed around in class when you were a kid. What did these notes contain? Heartfelt thoughts written to a best friend about your latest crush? A joke that only a young adolescent would find funny? Anxiety over the upcoming math test? In other words, nothing X-rated that would alarm a parent. Give your child the benefit of the doubt. Most of her e-mails are similarly benign.

Some parents understand that this correspondence should remain private and have other restrictions. "She has to get on the Internet through our password, which she doesn't know, so we sign her on," says one mom. "Once on, she has access to her own e-mail, which we don't read." Another parent says, "I go over and ask what she's doing and who she is talking to." Still another parent adds, "I randomly check to see who or what he is writing by lurking over his back and he never hides anything when I ask."

Most middlers know they are being watched. "My mom is real sneaky, or so she thinks," says one girl. "When I'm on-line, she closes in to give me a hug, but I'm on to her. I know she is just getting close to see what site I'm on." Yet, an occasional glance seems less intrusive than constantly reviewing e-mail. Children want to know their parents worry about their safety. But these kids also want to know they have their parents' trust. Try to find a way to preserve that trust with your child.

A Brave New Cyberworld

There's an exciting world on the Internet, one your child is eager to explore. Like any new frontier, this has challenges and risks, as well as benefits and rewards. Remain cautious, but don't discourage your child from becoming cyber savvy.

Middler Cyber Dictionary

pir: parent in room

g2g: got to go

lol: laugh out loud

ur: you are, also can be your

bf: boyfriend

bff: best friend, not to be confused with bf

sup: what's up, or what's going on

nm: nothing much, not much, etc.

n2m: variation on nm, means not too much

ne1: anyone

y: why

cuz: because, also seen as b/c

oic: oh, I see

neway: anyway

wtvr: whatever

ttyl: talk to you later

ttfn: ta ta for now

bb: most commonly known as buh bye, also bye babe

Note: Middlers rarely use punctuation (except for the occasional question mark) when they correspond on-line. One young adolescent explained: "Punctuation is rude."

What You Should Do

Learn about the Internet yourself.
Take an on-line tour with your child.
Talk with your child about your expectations for on-line
   behavior.
Stress the far-reaching and long-lasting effects of the
   Internet.
Talk about the dangers that exist in cyberspace.

What You Should Not Do

Constantly read your child's e-mails.
Radically restrict your child's movement on the Internet.
Underestimate the dangers that exist on-line.
Fail to report someone harassing your child on-line.

Chapter 5

Romance and Sexuality

"It's none of your business!"

When it comes to personal
relationships, parents' interference
can hurt more than it helps.

—Sixth-grade teacher

hose business is your child's love life? What about your
young adolescent's sex life? Your business, you insist. But is it?

Adolescents and romance are a volatile pair. In the infamous movie *American Pie*, a hidden camera in a teenager's bedroom plays a juicy, starring role capturing graphic erotic acts
and broadcasting the steamy encounters via computer to everyone in the high school's senior class. Such techno-capability is
not a Hollywood fabrication. There are cameras equipped with
sound and motion detectors that can be installed inside any

room in any home. Others can be affixed to automobile dashboards. So much for teen privacy on lover's lane.

As for futuristic chaperone gadgets, imagine the fireworks when a father confronts a teenage son or daughter with a hot and heavy video. Or worse, imagine your emotional state of mind if you caught your baby engaging in a sex act! YIPES!

Getting to the heart of a young adolescent's love life is a very sensitive journey, far more complicated than parents realize at the start of puberty. To discover whom your eleven-year-old son is (as they say now) "hot for," or whom your ten-year-old daughter has a major crush on is initially entertaining. Young lovers whose kisses risk tangling braces are cute. As middlers move further into the teenage years, in the mind of many a parent, a young adolescent in love is not cute. Your child and a paramour entwined on the couch is nothing to laugh at.

Not too long ago, at a breakfast for dads in Kentucky where we signed our books, a highly agitated father sought out our advice,

"Don't you think a fourteen-year-old is too young to date? My daughter, she's got this boyfriend, first love and all that. She wants to go out with him *alone* on a date. I say no. She is fighting me on this constantly. I know what's going to happen. I remember. She will have sex. What can I do to stop her?"

This father desperately wanted our agreement, as if our professional endorsement would add more weight to his no-dating policy, or finagle a change of heart on the part of his daughter. Fat chance.

For young and older adolescents, nothing rivals the pull toward affairs of the heart and the body heat such couplings generate. It's counterproductive to try to eliminate every romantic opportunity. Besides, the point of these years is for young adolescents to test out their adult wings, and that includes romantic, even erotic, wings. The idea of implanting surveillance devices is ludicrous. The ideal plan of action is to plant an intangible compass inside a middler's head, a compass that serves as a guide through romantic adventures. That's what this chapter is about.

In the following pages, we will give you strategies to protect your teen's coming-of-age romantically and sexually. We will provide a much-needed primer regarding romantic ideals and sexual intimacy. Certain taboo subjects will be illuminated. Guidelines on when to intervene will be included, too. The ultimate dilemma is how we can explain the positive and pivotal role of romance and sexual satisfaction in life while convincing our young to hold off.

The Code of Silence

The truth is that love, sexual intimacy, and erotic fulfillment—the triangle of entanglements—is *the most private* zone of all. On that statement, we and our young adolescents agree. Both factions conspire to create a code of silence.

As a New York parent confessed, "The junior prom is coming up. I know my daughter plans to stay out all night with her boyfriend. I don't want to know what the two of them will be doing."

Chances are the girl isn't going to come home and give a detailed accounting to Mom, though she might to a sister. For a parent, there is no honor—only danger—in such a laissez-faire stance. At the same time, if that mom assumes her daughter can "handle" the prom and all the pressures surrounding an overnight, she may be deluding herself big time.

Adults and their offspring ignore, rationalize, or try to camouflage what's happening in the intimacy department, especially sexual intimacy. Let's look at how each side conspires. At the start of early adolescence, children tend to spill details about the objects of their affection. Chances are things are pretty mundane at this point. However, as they get older, love and lust converge. They are maturing and learning discretion. And they pick up on parental anxiety. Revelations dwindle. The more a parent probes, trying to find out what's going on in a child's love life, the more a young adolescent hides. For adolescents, mum's the word on romantic and casual sexual encounters, often because what they are dabbling in is "forbidden."

"Do parents have a right to know everything about your life including your love life?" We asked. Overwhelmingly, our respondents wailed *no*. One thirteen-year-old boy insisted, "There are some things my parents need to respect—my privacy." Most likely these *things* are private pairings. Selective disclosure is typical, as this story illustrates:

"My fourteen-year-old daughter went away on a soccer trip for the weekend. On her way home she called me, using her boyfriend's cell phone. When I said, 'What's *he* doing there?,' she defensively told me he had come up this morning to cheer her on. I later found out (after interrogating the coach) her fifteen-year-old boyfriend arrived the night before and stayed in her room. I had not arranged for an adult chaperone in her room because she was supposed to bunk with teammates. The boyfriend told me his mother knew about his plans. When I called his mother, she had no idea he'd driven clear across the state. She thought he was at an overnight band competition. I feel my daughter deceived us. I think she planned this rendezvous from the get-go!

"My daughter and the boyfriend know our rules. I do not allow my daughter to date yet. These two have plenty of time together. He is always welcome to hang out at our house. We invite him along on family activities and outings. My husband and I worry about their getting sexually involved if they are left alone. Now I wonder: Have they?"

Parents become apprehensive because in their mind teen dating means only one thing: sexual activity. No sooner does a thirteen-year-old fall in love than a parent stresses out. The main objective becomes keeping the young lovers at arm's length.

Safety in Numbers—Parents' New Illusion

Experts endorse socializing in groups for young adolescents. Parents eagerly comply with what is akin to a *safety-in-numbers doctrine*. The unspoken rule becomes: Don't ever, under any circumstances, let a besotted twosome go out alone. No one-on-one dating.

The funny thing is that parents have pretty much succeeded in eliminating the date from the experience of early and older adolescents. Think about it. Fifth-graders party in groups at the movies or the bowling alley. They grow into adolescents who roam in herds about the neighborhood or through the mall.

Gone are the days when a tentative boy knocked on the front door, tripping over his feet (and his words) while he nervously brushed at the cowlick on top of his head. Dad interrogating, sizing up the suitor and his intentions—that's gone the way of soda fountain egg creams. Gone are the nights when sixteen-year-old Gidgets desperately stared at a telephone willing it to ring, screaming if her brother picked up the receiver to make a call. She waited for that special voice asking, "What are you doing on Saturday night?"

Nowadays, teens do not date. Boys don't escort girls to malt shops or drive-in movies on Saturday night. Girls and boys meet up at parties, at secret hangouts, at raves. Groups rule. Girls are more often than not the chasers in the game of love. As sweet sixteen rolls around, nearly everyone drives, has a sibling who drives, or has a car and gets to and from social events in cruising packs. Proms are not the exclusive venue for couples. Girls no longer play the passive roles of having to get invited. Anybody can go stag. Many do. Often friends accompany one another, no strings attached. Dating as we knew it is, for the most part, as extinct as dinosaurs. Kids don't miss what they never had.

Parents like it this way. When a child bucks the group trend and wants to date solo, parents get nervous. Mothers and fathers (like the one we met in Kentucky) may do everything possible to douse the twosome's odds. Negative statistics about teen romance culled from studies add to the antidating body of evidence. Lab rat Romeos and Juliets have been linked to increased rates of depression. Abusive romances have been documented, spiraling the victims into other disastrous syndromes such as eating disorders, suicide, and substance abuse. Parents read the statistics and feel even more convinced that nothing good can come from dating. Right? Wrong!

Falling in and out of love, getting rejected, or having a heart broken is turbulent for young teens. That's true. They are novices at identifying euphoric and catastrophic emotions. They do lack the skills to manage such extreme emotional sensations. Yet, by squelching the experience of dating for children moving through the teen years, parents deny young boys and girls not just the excitement of romantic drama, but the apprenticeship. They are prevented from selecting someone and creating a rapport, from getting to know that person in the realm of just the two of them. Instead they nearly always get stuck in whatever role they play in "the group."

According to Dr. Miriam Kaufman, a pediatrician, associate professor at the University of Toronto Medical School, and author of *Overcoming Teen Depression*, dating has benefits. Adolescents improve their social skills and acquire knowledge about the opposite sex. They gain exposure to new interests, like sports or hobbies. And a critical bonus, partners look out for each other during these years that are notorious for risk taking. She concludes that happiness is not the only thing to consider with regard to young love.

Yes, hearts do get broken. Yes, rejection does bring unhappy days and nights. Above all, though, dating is educational. Teachers we surveyed agreed. "There are things kids need to work out for themselves," one said. "When it comes to interpersonal relationships, parents' interference can hurt more than it helps." A guidance counselor added, "Children have to become advocates for themselves, and learn to get what they need from relationships. We have to teach them how to approach others for help when necessary."

Still, you can't stop thinking that a boy and a girl alone on a date invites sex. It is true that sexual experimentation is a feature of teenage relationships, the most incendiary for adults and adolescents to handle. But rather than spending all your energy and time putting obstacles in the way of your child's romances, a better stance is to prepare your child for romantically healthy relationships and the inevitable erotic road ahead.

Besides, just because there is no dating these days doesn't mean there's no teen sex. The safety-in-numbers doctrine has failed. There's plenty of sex happening.

Getting to Know Your Way Around— Helping Your Child Through

When it comes to sex and love, adolescents deny, deny, deny. They deny taking responsibility. Instead they opt for rationalizations. They feign not being ready for erotic encounters. It's become trendy to take chastity vows. Or to make promises of no sex to nervous parents, like this one. "My fifteen-year-old daughter has assured us that she wants to wait until she is married before she has sex."

Is virginity making a comeback? Yes and no. Many young and older adolescents are idealizing and pledging "virginity." However, that doesn't mean these same young people aren't intimately connecting with one another. They call it "hooking up."

To hook up means to pair off for the purpose of sexual experimentation. What kind of erotic experimentation? That all depends on the age of the hooking-uppers and their sexual readiness. Hooking up can be French kissing, oral sex, or sexual intercourse. The sex acts have little to do with age. There are twelve-year-old girls giving oral sex like good-night kisses, fifteen-year-olds sleeping around with anyone and everyone. The motivating force is age-old hormones and knee-jerk sexual attraction, not necessarily romantic infatuation.

When you broach the privacy zone of your adolescent's sex life, be clear when you use the word *sex*. What exactly are you intending to discuss? The act of sexual intercourse? Oral sex? Anal sex? The fondling of genitals? French-kissing? Are all of these "sex?" Ask your child to give you his or her definition.

In the last several years, an ongoing national conversation has danced around the question "What is sex?" Former president Bill Clinton wanted to go down in history as the education president. Instead he went down as the sex education president because of the Monica Lewinsky sex scandal in which he claimed oral sex is not sex.

A 2002 *USA Today* exposé screamed this headline: THE SEXUAL REVOLUTION HITS JUNIOR HIGH and uncovered an informational glitch. Young people aren't sure what constitutes sex. Thirteen- to fifteen-year-olds polled in the piece had trouble defining sex. Some said it had to be between a male and a female, involving a penis and vagina. What about the touching or kissing of genitals? What about same-sex sexual liaisons? Many said these weren't sex. Does that mean anal sex isn't sex? Does that mean sexual communion between gay or lesbian couples isn't sex?

Why all this hair-splitting? The answer can be summed up in one word: *abstinence*. A battle over including information about contraceptive methods and condoms versus teaching abstinence-only has raged in Congress. Legislators argue over which philosophy of sex education should be funded. The debate continues in classrooms and school board chambers in countless communities. As of 1999, nearly one in four public school teachers reported they taught about abstaining from sex until marriage as the *only way* to avoid getting pregnant or contracting a sexually transmitted disease (STD). This is a substantial increase from 1988 when only one in fifty sex education programs took the conservative approach.

While legislators and gatekeepers take the narrow sex education path, adolescents are all over the place erotically. Here are just a few glimpses:

- While 55 percent of teenage boys, ages fifteen through nineteen, reported having had vaginal sex, two-thirds admitted having received (or given) oral sex, having anal intercourse, or having the experience of being fondled or masturbated by a female, according to a study published by the Urban Institute in 2000. The survey was based on in-person interviews with 1,297 males, a national sampling.
- According to Dr. M. Joycelyn Elders, a former U.S. Surgeon General, and a professor emeritus at the University of Arkansas, there are twelve million sexually active teens who are nineteen or younger. More than 79 percent have had sex by age eighteen, and 80 percent by age nineteen.

- Child Trends, a Washington, D.C.–based research group, asked teens over fifteen if they'd had sexual intercourse by age fourteen. Yes, admitted 19 percent of girls and 21 percent of boys.

In a survey of Midwestern teens ages twelve through seventeen who received abstinence education, there was no consensus on what qualifies as abstinence. Youth meet abstinence with wily responses. They improvise. Technically, even if you've had oral or anal sex, or lots of fondling, you are still a virgin. Sex acts other than sexual intercourse have become popular because they are "defensible."

It's your job to counsel your child through the sexual terrain and through the "what is sex?" jumble. Where do you begin? Take these steps:

Discover the sexual mores of your child's peer group. Talk with your child about the sexual values of her peer group and other groups. But don't ask for the names of who is doing what to or with whom. You don't want to violate the trust you are trying to develop. Realize that this is not a one-time conversation. Start in middle school.

If your child is an A student, popular, or president of the student council, don't assume this translates into chastity. In the classic middle school caste system, the popular boys and girls socialize earlier and more frequently. While parents delight in seeing a child invited to parties and having lots of friends, they fail to draw the correlation that along with popular territory goes risk. More parties equals more exposure to alcohol and drugs. This leads to lowered inhibitions and more temptation to engage in sexual activity.

Even if your child isn't popular, he could still be experimenting. The cool kids and the not-so-cool kids all have hormonal surges and urges.

Avoid euphemisms for sex. Don't tailor rules like "Don't do IT." Choose specific terms instead. At first talking about intercourse or oral sex will feel awkward. It's worth the discomfort. When you distinguish between different sexual expressions, your guidance is more useful to a child. Let a child know that certain sexual forays are normal, natural, and okay. Making out, French-kissing, petting—gear your discussions about what's permissible to your child's age and *always* to your religious and ethical beliefs. Point out that sexual expressions other than sexual intercourse, namely oral sex and anal sex, do carry risks. Sexually transmitted diseases can be spread by oral and anal sex.

Don't burden girls with the entire yoke of lust. Don't fall into the double standards of sexuality. Where sexual responsibility is concerned, many of us harbor a subtle double standard without realizing it. During our years as on-line experts for several parenting sites, including Time Warner's ParentTime and iVillage's Parent Soup, we got a virtual earful of dilemmas.

"My son wants the Playboy Bunny icon on his birthday cake. Is this a BIG deal? I don't think so, but . . . Should he get the picture or not?"

The implication here is that a busty birthday cake cartoon is fine. The male sex drive is framed as fun, natural, urgent.

Often implied is its almost uncontrollable nature. Missing are sensitivity and the emotional part of sexuality.

On the other hand, girls rarely have their sexual desire framed so freely. Furthermore, the attached corollary to *boys will be boys* is that it's the girl's *job* to keep the boy in check sexually speaking. This presents trouble for girls. Their own sexual desire is not nurtured and encouraged as natural or equal, as legitimate. Their role is *not* to focus on their own sexual pleasure but mainly to red-light the male's desire. That is not fair. A girl is entitled to view her sexual urges independently and to value her sexual desire apart from how it arouses boys. Permission to act should be a separate issue.

Carefully note how you advise and treat the boys in your family compared to how you advise and treat the girls. Does an older brother live curfew-free? Do you tell him, "Keep on eye on your sister." Both you and he know that means he's the appointed sexual police. All this sounds like a great format for a family discussion involving you and your spouse and any young and older adolescent siblings.

Call an excuse an excuse. Underline that excuses don't cancel out sexual experiences. The Henry J. Kaiser Family Foundation surveyed 1,200 young adults between the ages of thirteen and twenty-four about their experience with partying and sex. Teens who drink are seven times more likely to have sex; teens who take drugs, five times more likely. *Seventeen* magazine published some telling responses from those over fifteen: 40 percent of guys and 32 percent of girls admitted that alcohol or drug use influenced them to do something sexual. One-quarter of fifteen- to seventeen-year-olds said they did more sexually than they planned to do because of drinking or using drugs.

Apparently boys may be gung-ho about sex, but many are still insecure. Nearly twice as many boys (19 percent) compared to girls (11 percent) turned to drugs or drinking to make themselves feel more comfortable with a sexual partner. Performance anxiety starts young.

Why the booze or drugs before the hooking up? The surveyed teenagers believed that if you were under the influence, you weren't culpable for your behavior. A girl nervous about her reputation could blame the alcohol, exonerate herself. A drunken Lothario can claim the encounter meant nothing, pointing the finger at the drug or drink for lowering his inhibitions. Thus, a teen can have sex and not be expected to call it a relationship, much less call the next day.

Discuss this blame game in your family. Ask if your children see it being played out. Agree that a person is still left with the history and the consequences, regardless of excuses. Those consequences can range from a changed reputation, to hurting someone, from contracting a STD to being date raped. Calling a rationalization a rationalization empowers your young adolescent sexually by teaching responsibility for sexual choices. If you are going to engage in oral sex or sexual intercourse, you must be man or woman enough to own the responsibility.

Know what sex education strategy and policy are being taught in your school district. The curriculum comes from state mandates and local school board philosophy. Many school boards narrowly define sexual education with an abstinence-only curriculum. No instruction about birth control or condom use is featured. Other schools include all aspects of protection and contraception. Some high schools make condoms available. What stance prevails in your community? Until you know exactly what your child is learning, you are not informed sufficiently to fill in any gaps. Only then can you insert your religious values and your parental warnings.

We want you to keep these facts in mind: Approximately four million teens will get an STD each year. Nearly half of teens did not use condoms in their most recent sexual encounter. Chastity-vowing teens are less likely to use condoms when they slip up in the heat of the moment. So while it is understandable for parents to endorse abstinence before marriage, pay heed to this remark from former surgeon general Dr. M. Joycelyn Elders, "Our statistics show that the vows of abstinence break more easily than latex condoms."

Frankly discuss the contraception issue with the teenagers in your home. State your opinions loudly and often. However, realize that your child's desire for privacy may affect what happens in the contraception area. Ask yourself: if your son or daughter opts to become sexually active would you assist in helping get contraception?

A 2002 Wisconsin study of 950 sexually active girls (ages twelve to seventeen) revealed that 47 percent would stop going to family planning clinics if their parents knew they were seeking contraceptives. Another 12 percent admitted they would postpone getting tested for pregnancy or STDs. *Meanwhile 99 percent of the girls who would stop going for services would continue to have sexual intercourse.* This study done at thirty-three clinics forecasted that going over the heads of girls to parents would translate into an increase in unintended pregnancies, abortions, out-of-wedlock births, and probably more cases of sexually transmitted diseases.

Supervise. It's easier than you think to pick up information once you learn where to zero in properly. Keep your ears open. You will learn where the "parking spots" are even though they are no longer called that. Ditto with the "safe houses for sex." As one parent reported, "Our town has a large community of summer residents. During the summer months many of the vacation homes are vacant during the weekdays and used only on the weekends. My sixteen-year-old daughter told me her new boyfriend can't wait till the summer. It didn't take a rocket scientist to figure out what he was thinking: so many empty houses, so many afternoons of summer love."

Don't overlook the obvious. Most adolescents get into sexual trouble in their own backyard, namely your home. Don't leave two besotted sixteen-year-olds home alone. Debate and establish rules about your teen entertaining a boyfriend or girlfriend in the bedroom, or watching TV together in the basement. Yes, rules are made to be broken. So the best insurance is to educate your middler, remain reasonable, and become approachable about the facts of life.

Calculate your child's readiness for romance and sexual exploration. As this mother pleads, "My daughter is nine but she thinks she is sixteen. Lately, she's obsessed. At day care today she got into trouble for playing a game with a friend. They called it 'Let's go to my boyfriend's house and have sex.' She is already developing. We did our first bra shopping this summer.

She is very interested in makeup. We've compromised on kiddie glitter body gel for the moment. She hasn't started her period yet. She's gone from Barney to Britney Spears overnight and I can't find the pause button. Help!"

Make peace with the fact that you are never (repeat never) going to be ready to welcome a child's active interest in sex. Commiserate with your spouse or other parents. Then get over it. Pledge to talk with your child about sexual issues. Enlist older siblings to help you get appropriate messages across. If you don't know what to say, get a good book to get you started. Our book, *Parenting 911: How to Safeguard and Rescue 10- to 15-Year-Olds*, covers how to handle talking about sex, but any bookstore or library has other options. Lobby to get a program going at your child's school to educate parents on being good sexuality coaches.

Don't cop out on love and lust. Failure to communicate about sex leaves your child in the hands of peers. In the current social climate, young adolescents cruise socially in groups. Multiple partners (hooking up) is more acceptable in their eyes. Just because your child doesn't have a steady partner doesn't mean sexual experimenting isn't happening. Talk about broad experience, and the toll that promiscuity can take on a child's innocence, reputation, and spirit.

Teen People partnered with the National Campaign to Prevent Teen Pregnancy and conducted an on-line survey of three thousand readers. Some 80 percent of girls and 74 percent of guys listed their friends as their most frequent source of advice on sex and pregnancy prevention. One girl explained it this way: "There's, like, no way I could ever go to my mom or dad." Be the kind of parent a child can turn to.

Cover-ups—
What Red Flags to Watch for
and When to Intervene

Young adolescent boys and girls can get in over their heads romantically. For instance, a thirteen-year-old girl hanging with her sixteen-year-old sibling's crowd may do things she is not ready to handle emotionally. And you can't expect older siblings to discipline or take responsibility for decisions made by younger ones.

That's just one example. In such situations kids may try to hide the details of their trysts or smother their mixed-up emotions. All middlers run risks. There is the jealous boyfriend who can intimidate. A twelve-year-old boy's life can be taken over by an over-controlling girlfriend. If we heed the statistics, many leap into sexual activity unprepared and get whiplashed in the aftermath. An eleven-year-old girl is swayed by peers to give a boy oral sex. A formerly innocent child becomes sexually active. Confusion and shame are right behind. Take this mother's story:

"I learned my thirteen-year-old daughter had sex for the first time three months ago. She was supposedly staying over at a friend's house on Friday night. They went to a party. She told her friend her knee hurt from a basketball injury and so she wasn't going to sleep over after all. The friend went home. My daughter stayed all night at the boy's house. When I called the girlfriend's house on Saturday morning, the jig was up! In the course of a long confrontation, my daughter crumbled. She confessed to having had sexual intercourse because she was afraid to tell the boy no. She's a good girl, gets A's and B's on her report card, is on the student council, and active in sports. We talked a lot and now she says she will never be afraid to say no again."

Did this girl give off any signs her mother missed? Perhaps not. But most young people in trouble socially or sexually do. Beneath their efforts to keep you in the dark are certain red flags:

- A precocious interest in pairing off before peers.
- You caught her/him lying about her/his whereabouts, especially involving overnight plans.
- Chunks of their time are unaccounted for and your child bristles when you try and pin him or her down.
- Provocative clothing.
- Signs of depression including changes in sleep patterns, appetite, listlessness, sadness, anger, failure in school, and substance and alcohol abuse.

Normal sexual encounters can upset a middler or adolescent. Even more traumatic is nonconsensual sex. Date rape and abusive relationships plague many young female adolescents. Dr. Jay Silverman, director of violence prevention programs at the Harvard School of Public Health, reported in the August 2001 *Journal of the American Medical Association* that one in five high school girls experienced physical or sexual harm inflicted by a dating partner. Interestingly, this mirrors grown women's vulnerability.

Observe the quality of the romances your daughter experiences. Is the relationship happy for the most part or unhappy? Look for the red flags mentioned above. Don't assume that your son is immune to humiliating relationships. Be on the lookout for these:

- *isolation* Your child doesn't see her old friends or participate in formerly enjoyed activities.
- *jealousy* Your child tells you, or you notice, her boyfriend (girlfriend) is jealous. Frequent fighting is a tip-off. So are constant phone calls or pages from him. These indicate a controlling tendency. Be wary if your child begins to follow instructions on how to dress, style her hair, or how much makeup to wear.
- *clothing* Is your child wearing too much clothing, turtlenecks in warm weather for example? She or he may be attempting to cover up bruises or hickeys— the symbol of sexual ownership.
- *apologies* If you overhear too many apologies, your child's "I'm sorry" may translate into her being dominated by an overbearing, abusive teen.

You can never know too much about your child's heart and romantic mind-set.

Love Lessons Start with Parents

Can you prevent raising a flagrantly flirtatious child, or one at risk for precocious, promiscuous, or abusive behavior? No 100 percent guaranteed policy exists. Yet, the ultimate safeguard is to express love and show affection to your sons and to your daughters. Dr. Wyndol Furman, professor of psychology at the University of Denver, and editor of a book *The Development of Romantic Relationships in Adolescence,* points out this classic corollary: "Parents should give children enough time and attention so that they're not driven outside to find support."

We asked educators to give their opinion: Are today's parents too nosy or not vigilant enough? Both extremes are counterproductive, said our teachers. A too-nosy parent who tries to micromanage every move an adolescent makes may drive that boy or girl into a secret life. On the other hand, a lenient or distracted parent sends a child the message that the parent doesn't care. As one teacher from New York remarked, "Despite the fact that kids do need some privacy, most issues do require parental help and too many parents abdicate their responsibility."

Show interest in your child's social life, but not too much. Are we contradicting ourselves? No. Some parents get overinvolved with their young lovers. When your fourteen-year-old daughter falls for that nice boy from that good family with a good head on his shoulders, shouldn't you be supportive? We've heard from parents who go overboard endorsing a romance. They include a boyfriend or girlfriend every time the family plans an outing or takes a trip. They endlessly congratulate their child on her choice. Cementing a romance is not healthy. The teen years are for making choices and mistakes. If you are overly supportive, your child may feel pressure to stay in a romance. Or she may dump a nice guy to spite you. So don't fall in love with your daughter's boyfriend or your son's girlfriend.

Be interested, open, and instructive rather than invasive. Here's a useful tip from one of our surveyed educators. "It's the approach that counts. Parents need to not *demand* information or avoid asking. They should find creative ways to engage their middlers to share."

Reassure your child that you are always ready to listen. Be affectionate rather than abrasive. Rather than going ballistic and haranguing about the slutty, sleazy behavior of teens today, help your young adolescent find the balance between finding love and getting lost in premature sexual activity. Talk, talk, talk about how he feels about what's happening around him. Reaffirm your values so he can make wise decisions.

Taboos—
Solitary Sex

In our questionnaire, we did not poll young adolescents on the sexual details of their private lives. We designed no questions to elicit facts on, for example, masturbation. In our first book, though, *The Roller-Coaster Years*, we underscored how much easier it is to talk to daughters versus sons about emerging sexuality. Menstruation is much less embarrassing to broach than wet dreams and ejaculation.

Even without our probing, over the last five years the subject of masturbation came up regularly in the question-and-answer rapport we conducted on-line with parents. Masturbation definitely qualified as a frequently asked question (FAQ):

- "My eleven-year-old purges her soul to me at bedtime—a curse word spoken, spilled milk. In a very
  roundabout way she's hinted that she touches her-

self. I've tried to have an open and healthy reaction, telling her that it is okay and that a lot of people do this. Still when she whispers in my ear, 'Mom, I did the M word today,' I'm very uncomfortable. Is my nonchalance correct?"

- "My sixteen-year-old daughter confessed to me last night that she masturbates. I tried to hide my shock that she would tell me this! Meanwhile I searched myself for the RIGHT answers. She relayed a conversation the kids at school had. A boy asked the girls if they masturbated. All the girls said no, even my daughter. She says it seems that in society it is okay for guys but taboo for girls. She thanked me for not being angry with her. I could tell she felt relieved, but what guidelines do I give? I'm thrilled my daughter has enough trust in me to share like this. Of course, tomorrow I will again be the Know-Nothing in her eyes."

Young adolescents are uttering sexually explicit confessions and questions that we never would have mouthed! They are much more candid than generations before. Sometimes their casual openness is stunning, not to mention excruciating, to their parents.

After hearing from many parents on this issue, we realized something. A parent automatically assumes that a child is looking for "answers" or "guidelines." Take another look. Read the entries again. The adults reverberate with discomfort and insecurity, ironically mimicking their offspring. And yet, what are these frank and outspoken girls really looking for? Reassurance. Young adolescents who masturbate want to know that their behavior is normal, within the acceptable range of human behavior. What they want is your acceptance and love of their sexual selves. When you give it, they have permission to accept and love that erotic part of themselves.

To make this whole subject a little easier, we suggest you take a light approach. While researching a plethora of studies, literature, and books on sexuality, we found ourselves hysterical over a historical discussion of terminology with regard to masturbation included in the 1998 book *Venus in Blue Jeans: Why Mother and Daughters Need to Talk About Sex*. The authors, Nathalie Bartle with Susan Lieberman, note there are "457 words and phrases to describe male masturbation and, in stark contrast, only 20 terms for female masturbation."

The authors contrast the imagery. Female terms favor cooking analogies: "rolling the dough," "flicking the bean," "tickling the taco." Or they reflect the arts: "doing the two-finger rumba," or "playing the silent trombone." Male linguistics reflect more physical and violent imagery. There's a lot of bashing and beating as in "bashing the candle" or "beating the meat." Add to that "choking the sheriff," "flogging the dong," and "whacking the weasel." Boys apparently make war not love with "playing tag with the pink torpedo," "holding the sausage hostage," and "doing hand battle with the purple-helmeted warrior of love."

If you are not laughing out loud yet, get a copy of this book and keep reading. Sharing this masturbation name-game with your child is a surefire way to get the two of you giggling past your discomfort. After the laughter ebbs, what remains is a foundation you have built with your child. You have scaffolded over an extremely private issue. Having that foundation is precedent-setting. Your child now has a rapport history, a framework with you characterized by ease. Next time he finds himself in a sexual quandary, it will feel natural for him to turn to you.

Still Taboo—
It's Still Not Easy Being Gay,
Lesbian, or Bisexual

Homosexuality seems to be out of the closet more with every passing year. Researchers eagerly and unabashedly pursue and discover clues to the biological destiny of those who grow up gay or lesbian. A 2000 study publicized in the journal *Nature* suggested a provocative piece of the puzzle. At a San Francisco street fair, 720 adults had their index fingers measured. In heterosexual typical males, the index finger of the right hand is shorter than the ring finger; in heterosexual typical females the two (index and ring finger) are equal. Lesbians' hand configurations turned out to be closer to the male model with shorter index fingers. This suggests higher levels of male sex hormones in early life. The index finger comparison didn't correlate at all to homosexuality among males.

Another study done at Berkeley by psychologist Marc Breedlove found a link between brothers and the likelihood of being gay: the more older brothers a male has, the higher his odds of being homosexual. Theoretically a mother's body remembers how many sons she's had, and she exposes each successive male fetus to more and more androgen. Breedlove recommends caution about these links. "There are plenty of gay men who are first-borns, and many women whose fingers give no clue. This is not a test to be used on friends and neighbors."

Some of America's favorite celebrities are gay. TV sitcoms like *Will & Grace* chronicle the comic foibles and tragedies of gay characters. Both reality shows such as MTV's *Real World* and dramas like *Dawson's Creek* zoom in on gay and straight melodramas with equal screen time. Ellen DeGeneres hosts *VH-1 Divas* night as just another comic diva. Rosie fights for the rights of gay and lesbian parents.

While it is true that gay, lesbian, and bisexual issues and people have more visibility and seem more commonplace, it doesn't follow that it is easier for a child who harbors a gay, lesbian, or bisexual secret. During adolescence the issue of sexual identity is as confusing as it is compelling. Being "different" as in being gay or lesbian is a liability. It is the major theme of ridicule in the peer culture of middle school, the number one insult. The typical high school student is within earshot of anti-gay insults twenty-five times a day.

Many ten- to fifteen-year-olds worry and question whether or not they are gay because they are attracted to a same-sex friend or adult. Helping children discover their sexual orientation, defining it, and raising tolerance are issues rarely broached in schools or at home. There are some school districts that introduced gay, lesbian, and bisexual support clubs but more often than not these become community controversies.

Statistics illustrate that gays are not only unwelcome in school but that half of an estimated annual population of

125,000 homeless teenagers confess they were exiled from family because of their gay and lesbian sexual orientation.

It isn't easier to come out these days. After the Matthew Shepard tragedy in Wyoming, many of us assumed that gay, lesbian, and bisexual teens would be safer, not the target of hate. Alas, this is not true. On June 21, 2001, a sixteen-year-old gay Native American boy was murdered, his body dumped in Cortez, Colorado. This town is just five hundred miles from Laramie, Wyoming, where Matthew Shepard died. The case bears too many similarities to the Shepard tragedy. Small humiliations and fear of heinous hate crimes still make a child fearful with regard to sexual identity.

Parents of all young adolescents—not only mothers, fathers, and stepparents who wonder about their child's sexual identity—have a responsibility to contribute to the climate of respect and equality for this minority. Only when it is safe to be gay will a child feel 100 percent confident to divulge his secret. Only then will the isolation that tortures many gay and lesbian adolescents no longer be necessary.

As it turns out, families throughout the United States have an enormous opportunity to establish tolerance. According to 2001 released census data that the federal government claims is the most thorough count of homosexuals in the population in the history of census-taking, a gay or lesbian couple leads a household in nearly *every county* (99 percent) in America. There are 594,391 same-sex-couple homes in fifty states and the District of Columbia, ranging from metropolitan areas in New York and California to rural parts of the Midwest and Deep South. "The census figures will change the debate for many Americans—from an abstract controversy read about in newspapers or seen in noisy debates on television to a discussion about real families, real people, and real lives," says David Smith, senior strategist for Human Rights Campaign, the country's largest advocacy group for gays and lesbians.

You can either accept these families or gossip about this tiny portion of our country's families. You can condemn them to pariah status or befriend them. What we all do individually and collectively affects the intimate privacy zone of the next generation.

If you are not capable of feeling tolerant about homosexuals as a group or if you feel anxious about the prospect of your child's gay, lesbian, or bisexual future, turn to Parents, Families, and Friends of Lesbians and Gays (PFLAG). This national organization has resources and support groups dedicated to helping everyone feel more comfortable with this minority. Its Web site is www.pflag.org. E-mail at info@pflag.org. If you have questions about your child's orientation, educate yourself for the well-being of your young adolescent.

Too Much Information— Too Little Too Late

If you feel as if you are fighting a losing battle in the war against sex, you are not alone. You are saying *no* or *wait* while the rest of the world is pushing *yes* and *now*. Adults are in the prohibition business. They warn about the risks of sex and the downside of unwanted pregnancy and sexually transmitted diseases. The media takes the promotion route. The musical soundtrack that scores teen life gets more risqué every year. *Thong, tha thong, thong, thong.* Lyrics talk about banging on the bathroom floor, and endless other examples. Fashions and fashion magazine spreads, TV advertisements, programs— you get the drift. When Britney Spears sang about not being that innocent, she spoke for an entire generation of our children.

Now before you wring your hands and give up, let me insert a sixteen-year-old girl's defense. "I don't see what you are talking about. Music's always been sexual. Remember. 'Please baby go all the way,' and the Beatles singing about doing IT in the road. 'Let's Get It On.' Come on, Mom." Neither the sixties nor the seventies boasted restraint, except maybe in the case of Jack on the TV sitcom *Three's Company.* He only pretended being gay. Still, the world our children come of age in is sexually charged.

While there is constant talk about sex, there is infrequent mention of romance and emotional intimacy. In other words, explaining the context of sexual expression gets short shrift. Parents get so wrapped up in the physical aspects of preteen and teenage romantic entanglements they lose sight of the emotional side. Or they think only in terms of heterosexual matches and never imagine the homosexual, gay, or lesbian possibility.

That emotional landscape of all sexual encounters is mind-boggling to young adolescents. Obsession. Need. Frustration. Rejection. Shame. Communion. Jealousy. Anger. Our preadolescent and teenage romantics ride no less than a *feelings roller-coaster.* They are getting little information on how to master this psychological whiplash. Add to that the paucity of romantic idealism in the current hooking-up culture of early and later adolescence. Doesn't anybody fall in love anymore?

Children need to understand romance and sexuality at younger and younger ages. *Teens Before Their Time*, a Girl Scouts of the USA national study focused on girls' views of issues in their lives, namely body image, relationships, and the future. Using focus groups and on-line polls for girls ages eight to twelve from 1999 into 2000, the data retrieved showed that girls are accelerating both physically and cognitively, but not emotionally.

Theirs is a world where fourth-grade girls, ranging from naïve to precocious don belly-baring tight tops to attract boys, slather themselves with makeup, launch popularity contests, and embrace partying beginning in middle school. Theirs is a culture where drinking is cool, where giving boys oral sex is commonplace by at least some girls. How do they manage fitting into this climate—a universal desire—and feeling good about themselves? Their plight is to understand their feelings toward the opposite gender and how that gender operates. The report emphasizes the importance of providing girls with a nurturing and safe environment in which they can discuss these concerns openly, hear honest and appropriate insights, and get guidance.

A place to begin is to inquire at school if any curricula in the sex education umbrella focuses on emotions, on sexual pleasure, and on how these play out in interpersonal relationships. If nothing exists, think about how you would teach the valid connection of emotions and sexual activity. Bring up your concerns to the school administration and the parent/teacher association. You may not be able to change the sex education format, but you may be effective in bringing in speakers or generating workshops for children to explore this important link between sexuality, feelings, and relationships.

What About Your Sexual History?

Should you share your own past sexual escapades, your end-of-virginity episode, the alcohol or drug-laced sexual lessons you learned in your younger days, with your teenage or preteen children? Is this personal information useful or not? Some parents insist on sharing so their children will not make the same mistakes. Others fear that admitting racy pasts will somehow give permission.

To spill or not to spill is a colorful debate, one we have moderated again and again with adults from the sixties, seventies, and eighties in cities, suburbs, and rural communities. In *The Roller-Coaster Years*, we spent an entire chapter called "Handling the Sticky Questions About Your Past," weighing the pros and cons. We repeat our caution: "Sharing secrets about the past may forge a bond, but at what cost?" Will you lose your child's respect? Will your authority be compromised? In the end, every parent has the right to confess secrets or not. Think long and hard before you do.

The love-and-lust privacy zone is the scariest of all. Our society has been described as in a national state of sexual arousal. That description pretty much applies to adolescence. During the patch when your son or your daughter can't think straight with hormones calling the shots, you have to insert your influence and a watchful eye. Ditch the futuristic cameras and do it the old-fashioned way. Talk—even though it's hard and uncomfortable work.

What You Should Do

Accept your middler's interest in sexuality as healthy and normal.

Encourage a dialogue on the social life of your child and his or her group.

Take responsibility for talking about sexual issues and decision making.

Show your middler love and affection often (though not in front of their friends).

What You Should Not Do

Take a totally negative stand when your middler shows interest in the opposite sex.

Pressure your child to reveal all the details of her social life.

Avoid broaching sexual issues because of your discomfort.

Show your middler's romantic partners too much support and affection.

Chapter 6

School

"It's my homework! You don't need to see it."

My mother's gone through my backpack and
it makes me mad. I mean, maybe I have
a test in there that I got a zero on. I want
to explain it to her before she sees it.

—Twelve-year-old boy

Remember those days when your child raced out of school
and proudly showed you the drawing he completed in class? Or
the many times your daughter eagerly displayed her spelling
test with 100 percent marked boldly in red?

Those moments are long gone. Your refrigerator door, once
a bulletin board for your child's academic triumphs, now holds
outdated wedding announcements, worn recipes clipped from
the newspaper, and invitations to last year's church supper.
Your child's schoolwork is found in the garbage can or crum-

pled in the bottom of his backpack. From day to day, week to week, you have little idea how he fares in class. Reality bites when that first phone call, parent-teacher conference, or interim report arrives.

Stunned, you may vow not to be misled again. If your child won't update you on his progress, can you get to the truth another way? Should you search his backpack, look through his desk, check his waste can, even pull up his computer files? Be careful. Those tactics may backfire, causing your child to become even more secretive and uncooperative. If your goal is to help him succeed in school, there are better ways to reach that goal.

In this chapter, we will give you strategies for supporting your child's education without becoming an academic police officer. In their own voices, middle schoolers will confess why they resort to subterfuge where their schoolwork is concerned. And teachers will weigh in with how parents can help, not hurt, their children's efforts.

You will learn why children flounder when they enter middle school. What are the warning signs that call for serious intervention and when should you hold off? We will sort through the various scenarios to give you pointers.

The middle school years are an important step in your child's educational journey. Your primary role as a parent is allowing him to own his work. While you should be available to help, encouraging him to take responsibility for his work will get him started off on the right foot. You also want to send the right message that learning, intellectual curiosity, is more important than his grades. Accomplishing that balancing act takes skill and patience. If you play your part well, so will your child.

Managing Middle School

Most children go through a transition period when they enter middle school. Your child probably will, too. Don't panic. The majority of students are able to adapt fairly quickly. Others may need more time, even some outside help, before they finally get with the program. Here are some things to remember:

Work becomes more difficult. Your child's learning picks up steam in middle school. The curriculum from fifth through eighth grade is designed to prepare your child for high school, college, and beyond. There is heavy emphasis on skills development— taking notes, preparing for tests, writing papers, and managing time. The memorization required for English vocabulary, a foreign language, history dates, and scientific definitions, is daunting.

Accountability is stressed. Middle schoolers are supposed to be taking responsibility for their schoolwork. Teachers advise parents to limit their involvement. No more typing that composition or constructing that science project. Doing so will make your child depend upon you rather than herself to get her work done. Unless you plan to attend high school and college with her, as well as following her into the workplace, this pattern is not one you want to establish.

The social scene kicks in—big time. As you learned in chapter three, friends become all-important in middle school. Middlers go to school not to learn but to be with their friends. What the teacher is writing on the blackboard is less interesting than what is written in that note being passed to your child by a friend. No surprise, then, that learning often takes a backseat to socializing. Lockers, changing classes, seeing different students—all these events are pretty new, exciting, and distracting.

Cliques and bullies torment others. Middle school operates on a caste system with the popular students ruling the roost. Unfortunately, cool kids often use cruel tactics to stay on top. If your child is teased, tormented, humiliated, or ignored, going to school may become painful, concentrating in class, impossible. Similarly, if your child becomes the cool kid, social pressure may derail her.

Puberty causes moodiness. Young adolescents are raging cauldrons of hormones. That chemical imbalance makes them irritable, forgetful, tired, and moody. Some children navigate these emotional seas well; others are in danger of developing depression, eating disorders, or substance-abuse problems.

Learning disabilities surface. Learning roadblocks, which could impede a child's ability to absorb, process, and retrieve information, emerge in middle school. Your child may have sailed through grade school, but with the work becoming more complex, he will find it harder to compensate for learning deficits. Because middlers are self-conscious, they may hide their difficulties rather than seek out help. Parents need to be proactive and intervene.

Circuits become overloaded. Because of everything going on in their lives—an increased workload, physical development, social maneuverings, friendship battles, increasingly competitive sports—young adolescents often become overwhelmed. Distractions are everywhere; staying focused is a challenge.

The complexity of middle school may catch your child off-guard. She, like so many of her classmates, excelled in the lower grades. Why is she struggling now? She is apt to become paranoid about her academic abilities, hiding her grades even from her peers. She's not alone. In fact, one case, in which a teacher had students grade each other's homework, made it all the way to the Supreme Court. A mother in Owasso, Oklahoma, filed the lawsuit claiming that the classroom grading practice embarrassed her children and was an improper release of their education records.

For your child, the only thing more frightening than having a friend see a failing paper is showing it to you when he gets home. Your child craves your approval. Worried that you may not understand why his efforts fall short, he will do everything possible to hide the truth. Coincidentally, in middle school academic achievement often becomes "uncool," giving your child further reason to avoid addressing his issues.

These tactics are universal among middlers. When asked in our survey if they ever held back information from their parents, the majority of young adolescents said yes, identifying schoolwork as a frequent subterfuge. A thirteen-year-old girl spoke for many young adolescents when she explained: "I am sometimes afraid of my parents' reactions. Maturity and trust play a major role in our family, so if I ever did anything horrific, their high expectations of me would be ruined."

Other students chimed in:

"My mother would be mad if she found out I got a seventy-five on my history test," said an eleven-year-old girl.

"My parents would be shocked if they knew I got a C+ in French," another girl confided.

"I always hold back on my test grades when they are under 60 percent," confessed a thirteen-year-old boy.

"I had a test and told my parents I didn't have to study because it was a quiz," said a twelve-year-old girl. "I got a bad grade and didn't tell them."

You get the idea. Over time, those C+'s and 60s add up. When you receive your child's report card, you will probably be shocked and angry. Don't overemphasize grades but take them in stride. Doling out punishment or snooping can eventually backfire. A better strategy is to educate yourself so that you can educate your child.

Empathize with her challenge to do well in middle school. Learn the proper way to support her so both of you will be on the same side. Visualize the coach of a football team. He knows the field and the best ways to score. He stands on the sidelines giving guidance, but never gets involved in the plays himself. He praises his team when they score, and comes up with new strategies when they fall short. As a result, his players trust him and confide in him. That's the relationship you hope to create with your child.

Getting to Know Your Way Around

How well do you know—really know—your child's middle school?

Probably not as well as you knew his grade school. Back then you felt welcome in the classroom. You might have been a parent volunteer, organizing parties or spending the day working in the library. You spoke frequently to the teachers and other parents. You knew your child's daily routine, what he was learning, how much homework he had. Sometime during the day you saw your child eating lunch with his friends, participating in sports, or honing his computer skills.

In contrast, middle school seems less open to you. Your perception is not unusual. As part of the process for helping students "own" their work, parents are given a broad overview but not all the details. Some schools are more forthcoming with information than others. If yours keeps parents out of the loop, you may feel woefully out of touch, particularly if your child does not fill in the blanks.

The middle school movement, which began back in the 1970s, recognized that young adolescents learn differently and thus need classroom environments that cater to their needs. Typically, grades five through eight were housed together and the curriculum revamped to jump-start learning. (Even in schools that were grades K–8 or six through nine, administrators tried to follow the middle school credo.) Yet many middle schools, while giving lip service to the concept, have been slow to truly embrace new ideas.

"Middle schools that have not done well have not because they didn't implement the middle school concept, which is based exclusively on the realities of human growth and development," says John Lounsbury, of the National Middle School Association, viewed as the founder of the movement. "Kids learn best in an engaging environment where their voices are solicited and heard. A good middle school seeks to do that."

How does your child's middle school stack up? Your first assignment as a parent is to find out. There are specific criteria you should look for:

A collaborative environment. Middle schoolers need a lively classroom where the teacher invites their participation. Hands-on activities, where they can play a part rather than watch, hold their interest. Large classes with long lectures are deadly. Research has shown that young adolescent boys can't sit still for more than fourteen minutes, girls for sixteen minutes, without a break. If you hear from the teacher that your child moves around too much in class, doesn't pay attention, talks to others, is disruptive, and so forth, investigate how learning is taking place.

A lively classroom, however, should also be well managed. A federally funded study of 72,000 adolescents in grades seven through twelve released in April, 2002, found that well-managed classrooms helped children connect with their schools. This positive environment finds students getting along with one another, paying attention, and handing assignments in on time.

The National Longitudinal Study of Adolescent Health said that a student's "connectedness" to school is critical to his well-being. Those children who felt this bond were less likely to engage in drug use, violence, and early sexual activity.

A wholeness to learning. An integrated curriculum, where subjects intentionally overlap, is a tenet of the middle school movement. Some courses are team-taught (English and history are a popular pairing), and assignments call for students to bring together in a final project their knowledge from two subject areas. Your child may do research on a Revolutionary War battle, for example, and write a short story using for background the facts he gathered in his investigation. If science and English are linked, he may write a research paper on a scientist but also be graded on his use of language, proper footnotes, and bibliography. At one middle school, students studied the lives of the French impressionist painters in history class, created their own canvas masterpieces in art, and wrote a description of their paintings in French.

The best middle schools, however, strike a balance between studying the past and addressing concerns students face in their present lives. For example, diversity, a theme that runs throughout literature and history, can be studied with renewed relevance to current events.

Parental input in projects. A good middle school teacher assigns occasional projects in which parents can get involved. For example, your child comes home and says, "Tonight I'm going to teach you the difference between latitude and longitude." Her teaching moment will incorporate what she has learned in class. At the end, you need to sign off on whether she has explained her lesson well enough. Or perhaps your child's class will conduct a survey and gather opinions on global warming or cloning. You will see her interviewing skills firsthand and know what and how she is learning.

The guidance of caring adults. Advisory groups, in which your child can talk informally with other students and a faculty advisor, serve as a mini-family. "School has a role to play far beyond the academic role," says Lounsbury.

Your child should have a faculty advisor and feel comfortable enough with this adult to talk about any issues he is facing, inside or outside school. **Alert:** While certain privacy issues may apply, this faculty member could be your best source for any concerns you have about your child. Middlers will often be loquacious with other adults while stonewalling parents. "Kids find some issues embarrassing to discuss with their parents, so they lie to them," says one middle school teacher. "Sometimes another adult can help."

Ideally, your child's advisory group should meet several times a week in the morning. Of course, your child would be able to meet with his faculty advisor at any time to talk. Admittedly, some teachers are more conscientious than others. If your child spends his advisory group time doing his homework while the teacher deals with administrative tasks, then this valuable device will self-destruct.

Besides a faculty advisor, your child's school should have other professionals on staff—nurse, psychologist, social worker, to name a few—whose sole mission is the psychological and physical well-being of the students. These specialists are trained to spot adolescent problems like depression, eating disorders, and substance abuse. They serve as another safety net for your child.

Health programs. Unfortunately, school health programs have been declining in schools, victims of cost cutting and scheduling mania. Often lessons on nutrition, exercise, and hygiene are shoehorned into other subjects and therefore risk being lost in the shuffle. How does your child's school address health issues? A good school program should include: health services

for needy students, nutritious meal programs, physical education, counseling, and health education. The best programs also
include forums for faculty and staff to keep them up-to-date, as
well as parenting talks for parents.

School size, not classroom size, is critical. Parents have long
railed against large classes. Yet the atmosphere, rather than the
size, determines whether a child feels connected, according to
Dr. Robert Blum, the director of the University of Minnesota's
Center for Adolescent Health and Development and an author
of *The Longitudinal Study.* "It doesn't matter whether you have
twenty or thirty kids in a class," he says. "It doesn't matter
whether the teacher has a graduate degree. What matters is the
environment that a student enters when he walks through the
classroom door."

School size, however, is important. The study found that as
the size of the school increases, student connectedness de-
creases. Schools surveyed in the longitudinal study ranged
from a school with only forty-two students to mega-schools
with more than five thousand students. When teachers know
your child's name, she is more likely to feel adults care about
her. It's perhaps no coincidence that Columbine, the scene of
the worst school massacre ever, is a supersize school.

However, children do need lots of students to bump up
against. The study found the ideal middle or senior high school
has an enrollment between six hundred and nine hundred students. Below that, the school may not have the resources to offer programs that keep achievement levels high; over that,
connectedness suffers.

Scheduled time for downtime. Middle schools on the cutting edge understand that young adolescents often feel stressed out and need a time and place to unwind. Study halls, where students do homework, and lunchtimes, which usually last for only thirty minutes, do not provide enough of an interval for relaxation. "Middle schools would do well to provide something comparable with nap time in elementary school," says Lounsbury. Does your child's school have a known safe haven—the library, nurse's office, an advisor's office, a corner of the cafeteria—where he can go if he feels stressed or threatened? Does your child feel free to take advantage of this place without feeling ostracized?

If not, then his room at home takes on added importance. "A young adolescent needs a chance to come apart after a mad day being so involved with others," says Lounsbury. "Privacy in their room provides them with that." (See chapter one, The Bedroom.)

Reasonable disciplinary policy. Young adolescents are notorious for pushing the boundaries and making mistakes. Your child may experiment with smoking or drinking, but ultimately reject both. Middle schools that make allowances for youthful indiscretions are ones that come out on top.

Still, many schools, pressured by school boards, the community, and the parents themselves, are overly strict, believing that anything short of zero-tolerance will result in another Columbine. Your child's school should strike a balance between being strict but also empathetic.

In the longitudinal study, schools with overly strict policies left children feeling less connected. "We found that students in schools with those types of discipline policies actually reported feeling less safe at school than do students in schools with more moderate policies," Dr. Blum says.

For example, schools with zero-tolerance policies, which usually means a child caught breaking a rule for the first time is suspended, could do more harm than good. Also, who decides which crimes are more serious? Forty percent suspended kids who were caught smoking the first time, while only four percent gave suspensions for first-time cheaters.

You may discover after looking over the above criteria that you don't know your child's school very well. You will find that many of the cover-ups and white lies your child resorts to have their roots in what is happening in his middle school. In order to decipher the puzzle that is your child's academic performance, you need to be better educated. Don't let another day go by without bringing yourself up to speed. Here are some ways to accomplish that task:

Get school policies in writing. Most schools have their policies detailed in writing. Go to the main office and request a copy. If one doesn't exist, make an appointment with the principal to be briefed.

Know what your child is learning. The school's academic goals and curriculum are often available. Get a copy from your child's teacher.

Know your child's schedule. Find out when he has classes that require more homework. Which days are popular ones for quizzes and tests? Does he have a study hall when he can do homework or library time when he can do research?

Meet the teachers. You should attend parents' night, held early in the school year. If you can't attend this event, schedule appointments with your child's teachers to introduce yourself. Get an overview of what your child will be learning, the workload, and when you can expect written reports. Find out if there is an early warning system, in the event your child is not doing well. While you want your child to take responsibility for her work, some situations may be out of her control and you may need to get involved. Earlier is better than later.

Acquaint yourself with the support staff. Visit the nurse, school psychologist, library, and any other office you can think of. Collect whatever material is on hand.

Get phone numbers and e-mails. Whenever you meet a teacher or a member of the school support staff, ask how you can contact this person. Vow to use them only in emergencies, but have them nonetheless.

Volunteer. While you probably will not be asked to bake cookies and, in fact, your interaction with your child could be minimal, there are still times you can pitch in. These are golden opportunities to talk informally with teachers and other parents. You may not even need to talk, just listen. Some opportunities: helping out in the library, chaperoning a school trip, chaperoning a school dance, or selling baked goods at a fund-raiser.

Attend parent talks. Most middle schools bring in outside speakers to talk about adolescent development, social issues, substance abuse problems—to name a few topics. School officials are often dismayed at the low turnout for these talks. You work a long day and probably feel your time is better spent at home with your child. Yet the information you pick up at these talks, as well as the added benefit to meet teachers and other parents, will more than compensate and, in the long run, help you to parent better.

Changing schools. You probably gave little thought to where your child would attend middle school. It's possible his grade school automatically fed into his middle school. Should he stay? Do you have an alternative in the event you decide his middle school isn't up to snuff?

Home schooling is an option some parents have chosen. Of course, if you have the financial resources, an independent private school or a parochial school, where you would have to pay tuition, might be an option. In addition, the education act signed into law by President Bush in 2002 gave parents the right to choose a better public school for their children. However, finding a spot in an acceptable school could be difficult, if not impossible, with so many parents angling for those slots.

Don't be too quick to give up on your child's school. Join the parents' association and work with others toward change. Approach the task with a win-win attitude. Presented in the right manner, administrators and teachers may welcome your suggestions.

Cover-ups—
How to Spot Trouble

Now you know about your child's middle school. You ask informed questions when he comes home and still get back zip:

"Do you have homework?" *A shrug.*

"What did you talk about in advisory group today?" *"Stupid stuff."*

"Did you do any experiments in science?" *"I don't remember."*

"Were there any tests today?" *"Leave me alone!"*

Your antennae go up and you suspect trouble. Are you overreacting or should you be concerned?

While you may feel your child's reactions are unique, middlers are surprisingly unsurprising when it comes to keeping parents informed about school. Even the best students sometimes engage in cover-ups. Why? The urge for privacy once again kicks in. If your child could articulate his feelings (and if he felt he wasn't going to be punished for doing so), he might say: "This is my business, not yours. You don't need to know."

One mother tells this story: "I was away with my daughter on vacation and when we called home my husband told me her grades had arrived. He wanted to open them. She went ballistic! I was worried that she had failed something, but I respected her wishes and we waited until we returned home so she could open the envelope. She had straight A's! She proudly showed us the reports. Later when I asked her, given the great news, why she didn't want her dad to open them, she said: 'Because they're my grades and I want to see them first.' I understand her feelings and next time will pass her the envelope, no questions asked."

Of course, not all cover-ups have such happy endings. More often than not a child objects to a parent intruding because of bad grades, not good ones. You want to stay on top of things to help your child before that failing report card arrives. Here are some of the more common middler cover-ups and what you can do to penetrate the secrecy without resorting to subversive tactics.

"I don't have any homework."

Your son has been playing video games for two hours straight and you finally tell him, "Enough! Do your homework!" His response? "I don't have any," or "I did it in study hall," or "I only had a little and I did it when I got home."

With few exceptions, young adolescents detest homework. "I lied to my parents about finishing my homework because I knew I'd be punished," says a twelve-year-old girl. While the better students recognize homework as necessary for learning, anything that interferes with the main agenda—socializing with peers—is loathed. Occasionally, even an honors student will decide to skip that evening's assignment in order to watch a favorite TV program, talk on the phone, or IM friends on the Internet.

That said, a child who habitually neglects homework is headed for disaster. As the parent, you are regarded by the school as the responsible party. After all, you are in the home watching. Shouldn't you notice whether he completes his work?

As you know, that's easier said than done, particularly when faced with glib responses like those above. So, short of rifling through his backpack, how to you find out if that homework is really being done? Employ these tactics:

Assume he has homework. Rare is the night when a middle schooler doesn't have *something* to do for school. In the lower grades, it may be one work sheet in math or a vocabulary page for English. The goal is to help your child develop a routine for homework that will help him organize his time when the workload gets heavier. Homework usually counts for a certain percentage of the grade, so it's important.

Check his schedule. If it's Monday night, you know he will have a math quiz tomorrow. Take out his schedule and remind him. Did he really have a study hall? If not, how could he have done his work?

Ask for a rundown of what she did. If she can't remember, chances are it never got done. Give her the benefit of the doubt that she did forget. Tell her that tomorrow you expect a more detailed report. That should help her save face and give her the necessary time to actually do the work.

Request to see the work. Make it clear you aren't going to correct his homework. You just would like to see what he is learning. If he says he left it at school, ask him to bring it home the following evening and then make sure to follow up. If he stonewalls you, he's probably slacking off. You shouldn't ask to see his homework every night. That strategy is too intrusive. But the occasional spot check will keep him on his toes.

Inquire if you can help. Sometimes homework doesn't get done because your child can't do it or didn't understand the assignment and is afraid to admit it. Probe gently to see if you can explain what she doesn't comprehend.

Don't rule out substance abuse. Your child's agenda may include getting high rather than getting high grades. Marijuana, in particular, kills motivation. If you see other signs of substance abuse (refer to *Parenting 911* for more information), you will need to intervene quickly. More is at stake than just failing grades.

Put popularity in perspective. Some children get sidetracked by the social scene. Doing well academically may tag a child "teacher's pet," and doom her social life. A Temple University study asked adolescents which crowd they would like to join. Only one in ten chose the smart crowd. One-third wanted to be with the partyers, and one-sixth wanted to be with the druggies. Help your child put popularity in perspective. You want a balance. You want your child to have friends, but you want academics to be important, too.

Give him an assignment. If you truly think your child is lying and hasn't done his work, put him to the test. "Since you've finished your homework, you can come help me clean the garage." You'll be surprised how quickly he will discover he does indeed have something to do!

"I handed my paper in. The teacher must've lost it."

On the other end, the teacher is probably hearing a variation on "the dog ate my homework." Somewhere between home and school is a large black hole filled with the lost papers of millions of middle schoolers. You are perplexed. What's going on?

He didn't do the work. The most obvious reason is that your son didn't do the work and is trying to cover up his crime. Don't let him off the hook. Tell him he needs to make up the work and this time you will check it before he hands it in.

She is disorganized. Middle schoolers become so overwhelmed that many things, including homework papers, get misplaced. (You may have a whole list of objects—clothing, cell phones, books, CDs—your child is still searching for.) Help her establish a little order in her life. Make sure she has a comfortable, well-lit place to do her work. With her permission, clean out her backpack. (You'll be amazed at the detritus that has accumulated in the bottom!) When she completes her homework, encourage her to routinely place it in the front pocket of her backpack so she will know where to find it. As a further safeguard, make a photocopy of any important homework your daughter does or have her save the file on her computer. If the paper truly is lost, she will have a backup.

His work fell short. Why would a middler do the work and not hand it in? Some children struggle and have no confidence that what they have produced is up to snuff. Their thinking: better not to hand it in and be viewed as lazy than to hand in a bad paper and be viewed as dumb. A red flag should go up here. Your child may be grappling with a learning issue. Make an appointment to see his teacher to discuss what she has observed in class.

"I have lots of time. The paper's not due until next Friday."

You know from experience, however, that may not be true. The deadline may be in two days and your daughter is giving herself an extension. If she is right that the deadline is a week away, you still know that she should be doing some of the work now, rather than pulling an all-nighter on Thursday.

Review your information. Major projects, research papers, and compositions are often discussed with parents during orientation. Look back at the material you collected to see whether that's the case.

Ask your son to see the written assignment. If he doesn't have it, that alone will speak volumes. How can he begin to tackle a complicated project if he doesn't even know what he is supposed to be doing?

Help her make out a schedule. Time management is an alien concept to most young adolescents. They always think they have more time than they do. Sit down with your daughter and have her detail exactly what she needs to do to get the job done. Have her estimate the amount of time each task will take. Encourage her to be generous in these estimates. Over the next week, prod her to stay on course. You might even reward her with each step she completes—a trip to the ice-cream parlor, or a half hour on the computer.

Use peer influence in a positive way. If your son's assignment is a group one, suggest he have his partners over to work on it. Hand over the playroom, order pizza, and retire to another room.

"The teacher can't teach."

Your child brings home a failing grade on a test. You thought your child understood the material and are shocked by how poorly she did. You are also put off that she is placing blame on the teacher rather than assuming responsibility for her failure. Your first reaction is to punish her until she can recoup. Should you?

Don't overreact. It's one test. Every middle schooler brings home a bad grade at least once. If you rant and rave you will ensure one thing: your son will never again show you when he fails a test. You don't want your communication to suffer.

Go over the test with her. Calmly sit down and ask to review her answers with you. See if they fall into a particular pattern. Did she make careless mistakes? Was there one area she failed to focus on enough? Ask her what she thought she could have done better to prepare.

Analyze where he fell down. Here you might be looking for a learning problem. Did the test require heavy memorization? Were instructions given orally or written? Your child may have a visual or auditory issue. Was he asked to analyze material he read? Perhaps he had difficulty making that leap.

Ask to review her class notes. Note taking is an acquired skill. While tests often focus on material in textbooks, middle school teachers also place emphasis on what is taught in class. Your daughter may need to improve in this area. Suggest that she talk with her teacher about ways to keep up.

Consider test anxiety. Taking a test is stressful, even for adults. For a middle schooler, it can be overwhelming. Review some relaxation techniques with your son. One is to take several deep breaths before beginning. Encourage him to get a good night's rest the night before and to eat a breakfast that includes protein the morning of the test.

Don't dismiss criticism of the teacher. Hopefully your daughter's critique of her teacher is wrong. But if the struggles continue, you may need to investigate further. Talk with other parents. What have they noticed? Make an appointment with the teacher to psych out the situation for yourself. If you decide there really is a problem, decide whether you want to go over the teacher's head and talk with the department head or principal. If you do, make sure you are armed with specifics rather than generalities.

Present it as a life lesson. Face it: your child will encounter many difficult people—teachers, bosses, coworkers, room-mates—where his coping skills will be put to the test. He may have a personality clash with the teacher. Or perhaps she really isn't as skilled at her job as she should be. Help your child understand that working well with others, no matter what the obstacles, is an important life lesson.

Perhaps the teacher is less than terrific. Yet because of her age and position, she deserves your child's respect. Make sure his behavior in class reflects that attitude.

Taboo Invasions— Moves That Can Alienate Your Child

In your enthusiasm to be your child's advocate, you risk invading his privacy in ways that are inappropriate. Nothing is worth jeopardizing good communication with your child. Keep that uppermost in your mind as you review this list of actions to avoid.

Don't rescue. It's tempting, to be sure. That big science project is due tomorrow and your son will never be able to finish in time. You know this last-minute rush to completion is his own fault. After all, he did play Sim City for three hours last night. You can't stand his whining and crying and you know he will be stressed out in the morning (to say nothing of the failing grade he will bring home). Why not help?

Be careful. Pitching in will establish a pattern that you will find difficult, if not impossible, to break in the future. Rather than do the work himself, your son will depend on you to do it for him. You will send him the most damaging message of all, that he is incapable of doing the project himself. You will "own" the project, too—probably the worst invasion of privacy a parent can commit against a child. And don't for a minute think the teacher will be fooled. The grade on this particular project has less significance than the long-term message and pattern you will create.

Don't take sides. When we talk with middle school teachers, one of their biggest complaints is that parents are reluctant to hear criticism of their children. "Believe the teachers!" one teacher pleaded. Marching to school and going one-on-one with the teacher will bring your child's private issues into the open and make her a target for teasing and ridicule. Respect her right to deal with the teacher on her own. That lesson is one that will hold her in good stead throughout her life.

Don't search for missing papers. You may hit paydirt the first time you search your child's backpack. "My parents snooped in my trapper-keeper," says one thirteen-year-old girl. "They found tests and quizzes I got bad grades on and got mad at me." Next time, this young adolescent will find a better hiding place for those quizzes. What won't happen is that she will feel more willing to share future test results with her parents.

Don't belittle your child. Throwing around words like *dumb*, *moron*, *stupid jerk*, *lazy*, will send your young adolescent further into his shell. You may never get him to open up again. "Form a strong bond of trust with your child, so that no matter what, the child shares information with the parent," urges one teacher. "Don't laugh, judge, or make fun of them."

Don't overlook searches at school. Do you know what the school's policy is for searching a student's private spaces? Surprisingly, even some teachers who answered our survey were unsure. When asked, the most common teacher responses were: "Not sure," and "I don't know." Many teachers, however, admitted to having searched a student's desk or locker, even without knowing the school's stand on this issue.

Make sure you know what your child may be subjected to at school. Explain the school's policy to him. You may not be inclined to search his backpack at home, but the administrators and teachers at his school may feel differently. If contraband is found in his desk or locker (drugs, a weapon, etc.), he could be handed over to the police.

Too Much Information—
Parental Hopes, Adolescent Fears

It's no secret that parents have become more vocal in demanding that their children be better prepared academically. "Parents are getting more scared about high school graduation and college entrance and entry-level work, no matter where parents are on the socioeconomic spectrum," says Patrick Montesano, the president of the Academy for Education Development, a New York City–based organization that works with middle schools in several states. "Therefore, there's more pressure on the middle grades."

It's easy to ring the alarm bell. You pick up a magazine and read about the challenge children will face getting into a good college and eventually landing a job that will pay a decent wage. How can you not worry?

As a parent, you are told to set the bar high. So you figure that you need to motivate your child now, in middle school. When he brings home that math test with all the red marks, you greet him with: "How are you ever going to get into college with grades like this?"

Middle schoolers are already stressed out. Give your child some time to find his balance. While middle school learning is important because of skills development, colleges don't see middle school grades. Your child has plenty of time to get into the academic swing. Also, consider the message. You are only as good as a subjective grade from a subjective teacher says you are. Overemphasizing academics can lead to serious disappointment later in life. Stress learning and natural curiosity, not grades.

Try not to ask your child how other kids are doing. Middlers abhor this type of comparison. If your daughter got an eighty on her vocabulary test, how can she admit to you that Lizzie got a perfect score? Conversely, if her friend failed the test, your daughter will be unlikely to tell you that. Young adolescents are sensitive about friends. Your daughter may fear you will criticize her friend or tag her as a bad influence. Focus on your own child first.

Don't compare siblings. It may be tempting to hold a younger child to the high standard set by an older sibling. Such comparisons will have disastrous effects on both children and their relationship. Remind yourself that each child is an individual and should be recognized for his or her own strengths and talents.

Middle school will be a challenging time for your child.

Keep in mind that learning is a process. Expect the occasional disaster. Celebrate every success. You are your child's most important advisor. Make sure, however, that you remain in the role of coach. This is your child's game and, if you mind the rules well, you can be there cheering him on during his years in middle school and beyond.

What You Should Do

Know your child's school—its teachers, administrators, requirements, rules, routines.

Help your child "own" her work.

Teach your child organizational skills.

Volunteer at your child's school.

Encourage group learning with friends.

What You Should Not Do

Panic when your child brings home a bad grade.

Do your child's homework.

Blame the teacher for your child's woes.

Look for tests and quizzes in your child's backpack.

Get alarmed because of competition to get into college.

Chances are when you picked up this book, you were feeling left out. When you heard the expression, "the wonder years," you may have quipped, Yes, I am wondering . . . about a lot of things: What's going on inside my son's mind? Is my daughter worrying about her weight? Are my children walking through a gauntlet of temptation or humiliation at school?

Standing outside your child's bedroom door, tapping while asking, "Please, let me in," you know you were talking about more than just getting inside the bedroom. You, like most parents of ten- to fifteen-year-olds, crave access to your child's private thoughts in order to allay your fears.

When your son or your daughter acted less than forthcoming in the information department, you probably contemplated sneaky maneuvers to get the lowdown. Maybe you even read a diary entry or two, eavesdropped on a telephone conversation, or retrieved a crumpled note here and there from the backpack or wastepaper basket.

Now that you have finished reading, we hope that you have a different perspective and an effective set of parenting tools. As you have seen what we, what educators and parents, and what young adolescents had to say about privacy, you have become privy to many ways to get closer to your children respectfully. You can penetrate your child's private pleasures and passions and those secret fears and foibles without resorting to snooping.

We want to leave you with a wrap-up exercise. It is inspired by a parent, one of the thousands who gave us invaluable input over the years and demonstrated how smart parents can be.

"Here is a game I play once a year with my kids. We've done it for the past three years. It's a game of questions. Some of the answers may seem obvious, but if you take the time to answer the questions and then get the real answers from your child, I guarantee you that there will be surprises. And it's a fun way to get information that you may not know otherwise. It has taught me a geat deal."

We adapted what resembles the old *Newlywed Game* format, only this gameshow gimmick revolves around your love affair with your child and not your spouse. Ask away, even if your kids have been known to say, "Mom, you ask too many questions!"

1. What color would your child like her room to be?
2. What is your child's most cherished childhood memory?
3. Outside your family, who has influenced your child the most during the past year?
4. What subject at school rates "most favorite" and "least favorite"?
5. What is your child's biggest complaint about his family?
6. What gift from you or your spouse does your child cherish the most?
7. What nonschool item (book or magazine) has your child read recently?
8. What nicknames are attached to your child at school?
9. What is your child's most prized possession?
10. Of what accomplishment is your child most proud?
11. If you let your child plan a dream vacation, where would she go and what would the itinerary be?
12. What is her favorite meal?
13. What embarrasses him the most these days?
14. What pet would your child prefer: a dog, cat, bird, fish, or some other?
15. What is her favorite CD, TV show, and Web site?

If you kept a tally from year to year, all through adolescence, with each of your children, what an entertaining bit of family history it would make.

In our too-busy world, it's easy to lose touch and forget about some of the nuggets within these questions. This guided tour of queries will take you places that you and your young adolescent should go. You will feel like you know more. She will feel like you care.

Finally, always distinguish between what you want to know and what you need to know. It's not always the same thing. What you want is to corral, not control your child. What your child needs is supervision and space to grow into the person he hopes to become. What you both want and need is each other, perhaps the best kept secret of adolescence.

Index

About the Authors

Margaret Sagarese (left) is a former teacher and the author of thirteen books. She lives on Long Island, New York.

Charlene C. Giannetti is a journalist and the author of eight previous books, including *Who Am I? . . . and Other Questions of Adopted Kids*. She lives in New York City.